THE NIGHT
OF THE
IGUANA

PLAYS

Baby Doll & Tiger Tail

Camino Real (with *Ten Blocks on the Camino Real*)

Candles to the Sun

Cat on a Hot Tin Roof

Clothes for a Summer Hotel

Fugitive Kind

A House Not Meant to Stand

The Glass Menagerie

A Lovely Sunday for Creve Coeur

Mister Paradise and Other One-Act Plays:
These Are the Stairs You Got to Watch, Mister Paradise, The Palooka, Escape, Why Do You Smoke So Much, Lily?, Summer At The Lake, The Big Game, The Pink Bedroom, The Fat Man's Wife, Thank You Kind Spirit, The Municipal Abattoir, Adam and Eve on a Ferry, And Tell Sad Stories of The Deaths of Queens...

The Night of the Iguana

Not About Nightingales

The Notebook of Trigorin

Something Cloudy, Something Clear

Spring Storm

Stairs to the Roof

Stopped Rocking and Other Screen Plays:
All Gaul is Divided, The Loss of a Teardrop Diamond, One Arm, Stopped Rocking

A Streetcar Named Desire

Sweet Bird of Youth (with *The Enemy: Time*)

The Traveling Companion and Other Plays:
The Chalky White Substance, The Day on Which a Man Dies, A Cavalier for Milady, The Pronoun 'I', The Remarkable Rooming-House of Mme. Le Monde, Kirche Küche Kinder, Green Eyes, The Parade, The One Exception, Sunburst, Will Mr. Merriwether Return from Memphis?, The Traveling Companion

27 Wagons Full of Cotton and Other Plays:
27 Wagons Full of Cotton, The Purification, The Lady of Larkspur Lotion, The Last of My Solid Gold Watches, Portrait of a Madonna, Auto-Da-Fé, Lord Byron's Love Letter, The Strangest Kind of Romance, The Long Goodbye, Hello From Bertha, This Property is Condemned, Talk to Me Like the Rain and Let Me Listen, Something Unspoken

The Two-Character Play

Vieux Carré

Alan Webb, Margaret Leighton, Patrick O'Neal, and Bette Davis in the original Broadway production of *The Night of the Iguana*. (Photo courtesy of Friedman-Abeles.)

TENNESSEE WILLIAMS

THE NIGHT
OF THE
IGUANA

INTRODUCTION BY
DOUG WRIGHT

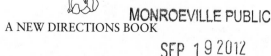

A NEW DIRECTIONS BOOK

Manufactured in the United States of America
New Directions Books are printed on acid-free paper.
First published clothbound by New Directions in 1961
First published as New Directions Paperbook 1156 in 2009
Published simultaneously in Canada by Penguin Canada Books, Ltd.

Library of Congress Cataloging-in-Publication Data
Williams, Tennessee, 1911–1983.
The night of the iguana / by Tennessee Williams ; introduction by Doug Wright.
p. cm.
ISBN 978-0-8112-1852-8 (paperbook : alk. paper)
I. Title.
PS3545.I5365N5 2009
812'.54—dc22   2009019755

10 9 8 7 6 5 4 3 2

New Directions Books are published for James Laughlin
by New Directions Publishing Corporation
80 Eighth Avenue, New York, NY 10011

CONTENTS

INTRODUCTION:
UNCLE TENNESSEE

My mother had a headache, and so I came to know the work of Tennessee Williams.

Dallas, Texas, is a more sophisticated city now, but in 1974 it was still a cultural backwater, and my parents were absolutely vigilant about exposing us to the intermittent art that came our way. The local university hosted an annual subscription series: for a modest fee, you could attend lectures, concerts, literary readings, and plays throughout the year. Eagerly, my parents joined.

Subscription nights were very special indeed. My mother would apply lipstick (something she rarely did), my father would come home from his law office on the early side, and together they'd leave my siblings and me in the company of our elderly babysitter, who'd turn on the TV, pop some Jiffy-Pop, and pray for the best. The next morning over breakfast, Mom and Dad would regale us with tales of PDQ Bach and his hilarious piano, or recount the thrill of hearing Garson Kanin read from one of his novels.

But one evening in the fall of my twelfth year, my mother announced that she was feeling peaked; it was one of her sinus head-aches. That meant that my father was saddled with an extra ticket. He could go by himself, or recruit one of the children. My brother was more interested in his model planes than art with a capital "A," and my sister was too young to sit still for two hours, so I was drafted.

Of course, I'd been to the theater before. I'd seen children's fare at the Junior Player's Guild, ranging from *Rumpelstiltskin* to *Frog and Toad*, and I knew Engelbert Humperdinck's *Hansel and Gretel* by heart. I'd even been to a grown-up play: *Life with Father* by Howard Lindsay and Russell Crouse.

But if my parents had known the bill that evening, they might have been more circumspect. After all, I was at an impressionable age. Still, they were progressive people, and I'm sure they reasoned that a night spent in the presence of a Great American Drama—*any* Great American Drama—was preferable to one in front of the idiot box. Why shouldn't they expose me to the canon early? It's never too early, is it, to instill a life-long love of literature? And that's how I came to see a touring production of *A Streetcar Named Desire*.

I don't recall the name of the theater company. I don't recall the cast. In truth, I don't know if it was a professional or an amateur production.

What do I remember? Decades later, I can still recall the image of Blanche, pristine in white gloves, entering the lurid world of the French Quarter as a jazz saxophonist plaintively wails in the night. I can't forget Stanley, crudely handsome, his chest bare, strutting about the stage like a prizefighter in a red silk robe that clung to his physique like Saran-Wrap. (It was the first time I'd seen a man as lovingly eroticized as the Playboy Bunnies I'd glanced at the drugstore newsstand; it mesmerized and terrified me at the same time.) Echoing in my ears, I can still hear the horrible cry of "Fire! Fire!" as our heroine, her hair now wild and loose, and her prim suit replaced by a disheveled kimono, tries to incite and suppress potential rape.

Most of all, I remember hearing music as recognizable and singular as Gershwin or Mozart, with as distinct and enduring a melody. But it wasn't born of instruments; it was borne of words. It was the same vernacular my grandmother used when I visited her in Springfield, Missouri ("You've such fragile, fair skin for a little boy," she'd say, or "It's the last dress I'm ever going to buy, pale peach, to match the lining of my casket"), but elevated to the level of poetry. It wasn't naturalistic; it was somehow truer. It conveyed the terrors and the pleasures of life with greater acuity than spontaneous speech ever could. And though the play was performed in a darkened theater for hundreds of spectators, I felt instead that it had been whispered in my ear by the author, imparted as a delicious and mortifying secret that only the two of us shared.

When I left the theater that night, there were three people in my father's navy-blue Lincoln Continental. Dad was in the driver's seat, I was next to him, and perched in the back, invisible except to me, sat a figure in a Panama hat and crumpled linen suit, with the slightest hint of liquor on his breath. During the play, he'd slyly implicated himself in my life; I knew he wasn't leaving anytime soon. He caught my glance in the rearview mirror. The wicked twinkle in his eye and the sad, wise cackle when he laughed carried a promise: he was my new Uncle. He would teach me all the reckless, impolite truths about life no one else in the confines of my hometown possibly could. Some would be salacious. Others would be too moving, too profound to bear. All of them would be well beyond the purview of my mom and dad.

Later that week when our art teacher at school assigned dioramas, I took a shoebox, doll furniture from my sister, and scraps of fabric from mother's sewing box, and built my own model of the Kowalski residence, complete with tiny beer bottles and a Chinese lantern fashioned from tissue paper. That same week, I stole an old bathrobe of my mother's and a stringy blonde wig from our box of Halloween costumes, and put them on, so that I could intone tragically before the mirror, "I have always depended on the kindness of strangers." When Mother poured me a soda pop one day after school, I flashed a coy smile and inquired coquettishly in my best antebellum drawl, "Is this . . . *just* Coke?" She just looked at me, baffled.

The next Saturday morning, when Mom took us on our weekly trip to the Public Library, I forsook the children's section. It's as if I heard Tennessee's velvety voice, urging me, "Over here. That's right. Come on over to *Modern Drama* instead." Stealthily, I crept past *Ramona the Pest* and *The Hardy Boys*, and into terra incognita: the plush, carpeted splendor of the adult wing. Plays were in the back, perpendicular to the wall, where no one would notice a gawky pre-adolescent sneaking his first peek at the farm-fed athletes of William Inge and the pensive, doomed women of Eugene O'Neill.

Uncle Tennessee had his own shelf, bowing in the middle under the weight of his plays. Each hardcover was alluring to me, as irresistible as Pandora's Box. What would I find inside? Hysterical spinsters, punitive daddies, achingly beautiful, damaged young men, bawdy widows, broken souls, redemption, damnation, and language as potent as laudanum or absinthe.

Despite the disapproving glare of the librarian, over the next few months, I pored through play after play. One weekend, it was *The Glass Menagerie* with tremulous Laura, her omnivorous mother, and the illusory promise of the Gentleman Caller. The next, it was *Orpheus Descending,* with Lady and Val locked in their fateful, erotic dance. Other kids at school knew the defensive line-up of the Dallas Cowboys; I could recite from memory the original production team of *Cat on a Hot Tin Roof.*

Was I precocious enough to understand everything I'd read? Certainly not. The more experimental work in particular (*Camino Real* and *In the Bar of a Tokyo Hotel*) might as well have been rendered in hieroglyphs. It didn't matter; to me, they were sacred texts and like all such volumes, their inscrutability was part of their allure.

When I ran out of plays, I turned to the short stories and the novels. Finally, brazenly, I attacked his autobiography. Critically derided as distastefully confessional, I found it purgative. His frank descriptions of male beauty, like the Canadian dancer Kip, whom he met on the beaches of Provincetown, were liberating. His tempestuous relationship with Frank Merlo felt like the first authentic love story I'd ever read. And the occasional night he spent in the arms of a one-night trick or hustler echoed the loneliness, the disenfranchisement, I already felt as a closeted gay kid in a very conservative state. In their candor and their heartache, his memoirs allowed me to confront my own burgeoning desire.

One evening when I was about fifteen, I noticed in the television listings that the Late Movie was a film adaptation of a Williams play I hadn't read. Its title: *The Night of the Iguana.* (My cousin Alan in Lubbock had an iguana that he'd carted up from a fraternity vacation to Mexico as a pet for a brief time. One day it escaped the aquarium where he kept it, and disappeared between the walls of the house. My Aunt Marylouise lived in terror of its sudden, unexpected resurgence through a vent or toilet. Suffice it to say, Williams's title bristled with promise.)

I had to watch this movie, but how? It wasn't airing until long after my bedtime. I knew what I had to do: wake up in the middle of the night, sneak past my slumbering brother, and barricade myself in the den, keeping the volume low so my parents wouldn't stir downstairs. Finally, the hour arrived. Alone in the dark, I turned on the set. The credits began to flicker in glorious black and white, and soon I was engulfed in the story of a group of charismatic misfits traveling through Puerto Barrio, Mexico.

I'll leave it to the critics and the literary theorists to discuss the abundant symbolism in *Iguana*, its place in Williams's oeuvre, its thematic intent, its impact on the Broadway season of 1961, and its relevance to contemporary culture. I can only speak about one thing: its impact on the adolescent mind of one particular boy, splayed on his rec room couch, late one night circa 1977. Once again, my dear uncle, as reliable as he was fictive, articulated to me the formative truths that no one else in my life dared to name.

Reverend T. Lawrence Shannon is the hero of the play; he's a defrocked preacher leading a bevy of Texas harpies through Mexico on a guided tour. He may have seemed like an exotic character to viewers less seasoned than me, but I pegged him right away. Growing up in the Southwest, I'd known plenty of clergymen torn between an unyielding belief in a punitive God, and an insatiable appetite for sex. If you were old enough to attend church, you were old enough to know about scandal. I understood, too, how he was both perpetrator and victim of his own stringent religion. He couldn't forgive himself for the tawdry affairs that had lead him to the brink of ruin. Self-recrimination was something I knew well. As a child, I spent many nights cowering under my bed sheets, with a flashlight and Bible in hand, reading feverishly in an effort to ward off my own homosexuality. (My parents were far from zealots, but in our community, fundamentalism was as pervasive as cicadas in June.)

I also recognized Miss Judith Fellowes and her brigade of Texas ladies. They might've been my elementary school teachers, prim ladies in sensible shoes and shellacked hair, who craved adventure but not inconvenience. (Years later, when I finally saw *Iguana* staged, I was heartsick to learn that they were John Huston's invention for the film, and were only referenced in the play itself.) These women are blind to their own hypocrisy; they crave a handsome, attentive guide, who will flirt with them incessantly, without ever revealing a vestige of sexuality in his personal life. I'd seen the same hungry look in the suburban mothers who clamored around our coach at junior high. (Rumor has it that Coach Nevermind subsequently lost his job for bedding down with a student; shades of the Reverend Shannon indeed!)

Even embodied by glamour-puss Ava Gardner, the character of Maxine Faulk was no mystery. I'd seen plenty of blowsy, over-ripe gals like her, who tousled their hair, hugged you too tight, and laughed deep down in their throats, like kitchen disposals. She reminded me of the waitresses at the Lucas B&B Diner, who'd flirt with me outrageously, exclaiming, "I've finally found Mr. Right!" as they topped my apple pie with an extra wedge of cheddar cheese. (A gawky, slightly effeminate boy like me made for an irresistible target.)

Only the spinster Hannah Jelkes was unlike anyone I had ever met. Traveling selflessly with her aging grandfather, living off the mercy of tourists who buy her sketch portraits, bereft of love but seemingly not made bitter by its absence, she was a complete enigma to me. I had no frame of reference, no ready categorization for her. Yet, she offered me something indispensable.

Near the play's climax, she finds herself locked in an all-night battle of ideological will with the fallen preacher. He's grilling her mercilessly about the lack of romance in her life, and she's driven to recount a brief, abortive affair with an Australian salesman. The Reverend judges their encounter as sordid, and asks her point-edly if she was disgusted. Her answer is simple, but startling in its humanity; she tells him "nothing human disgusts me unless it's unkind, violent."

When I heard those words, I felt a surge of sudden, unexpected tears. Her theology was far more empathetic than the minister's. That sounded like the kind of religion I could actually embrace, and yet I'd never heard it in church; I learned it from the midnight movie. In the person of Miss Jelkes, Tennessee Williams offered a gentle corrective to the mendacity, and provincialism, that so readily masqueraded as religious faith in my youth.

And Hannah Jelkes wasn't even clergy. No, she was something greater: an artist. In Williams's world, a portraitist with a poet father is a more reliable conduit for truth than a misguided man of God. Art, he suggests, is the closest thing we have to a collective conscience, far more than mere theology.

Now Uncle Tennessee had, to say the least, a checkered reputation. Especially in his later years, the world came to regard him as louche, even decadent; self-satisfied moralists clucked that his sorry decline was the natural result of his overindulgence and ab-errant sexuality. But make no mistake about it: he introduced me to grace. And by that I mean grace in the liturgical sense: the spirit of God as it operates in people to ennoble and strengthen them. I'm not religious *per se* but when I have divined God's presence, it's always been in a theater, and never more so than when I am watching a Williams play. When Blanche in *Streetcar* gasps, "Sometimes there's God so quickly," she might as well be referring to any number of epiphanic moments in the playwright's own work: when Jim christens Laura's disease "blue roses" in *Menagerie* or Serafina gets a second chance at love with Alvaro in *The Rose Tattoo*.

When Hannah and Shannon conspire to set the chained iguana under the porch free, I felt strangely liberated, too. I didn't understand the metaphor, not fully, but I knew that I could break loose from the confines of my family and my town, and forge my own future in the comparative wild, among my own kind: school on the radical East Coast, and an eventual move to that fabled Bohemia, New York City.

Years have passed, and now I am a professional playwright, if such a profession still exists. Many of my colleagues, Lanford Wilson and Edward Albee among others, actually knew Tennessee. I never shook his hand, or saw him passing on the street, or even penned a fan letter. I only have the imaginary uncle in the backseat. But I am not alone; I think every working American playwright claims a certain kinship to Williams. We write alongside him; he is our shared history.

But the debt I owe him is more than just collegial. I was a gay boy in the mid-seventies in Texas who wanted to write plays; I had no role models. Dallas had stayed mired in the Eisenhower fifties for most of my childhood; in our cloistered state of conservative denial, we'd somehow missed Vietnam, Stonewall, and the martyrdom of Harvey Milk. Even now, I thank God that my phantom uncle reached out across a university stage, through a library bookshelf, to take me by the hand. He had his imperfections, true; the wounds inflicted upon him by his family's baroque pathology, and the cruel age in which he lived. But he rose above them to achieve the expansive, generous and forgiving view of mankind that Christianity so often teaches and so rarely achieves. He was my first tutor in the fragility, the wonder, and the maddening contradictions of the human heart.

My partner David and I frequently spend our summers in Provincetown, where Williams enjoyed some of the most productive writing months of his life. Each year, I pay my own tiny homage to him; I visit a small photograph that hangs in the Little Bar of the Atlantic Guest House on Masonic Place, where he allegedly completed an early draft of *The Glass Menagerie*. The snapshot is black and white, and a bit grainy, but exuberant all the same: it shows Williams buck naked, flinging his arms in joyous exaltation, galloping along the sand.

When I pause before it, I am a distant nephew honoring his uncle. I am a pilgrim, venerating an unexpected Saint.

Doug Wright
New York City
April 2009

THE NIGHT OF THE IGUANA

The play takes place in the summer of 1940 *in a rather rustic and very Bohemian hotel, the Costa Verde, which, as its name implies, sits on a jungle-covered hilltop overlooking the "caleta," or "morning beach" of Puerto Barrio in Mexico. But this is decidedly not the Puerto Barrio of today. At that time—twenty years ago—the west coast of Mexico had not yet become the Las Vegas and Miami Beach of Mexico. The villages were still predominantly primitive Indian villages, and the still-water morning beach of Puerto Barrio and the rain forests above it were among the world's wildest and loveliest populated places.*

The setting for the play is the wide verandah of the hotel. This roofed verandah, enclosed by a railing, runs around all four sides of the somewhat dilapidated, tropical-style frame structure, but on the stage we see only the front and one side. Below the verandah, which is slightly raised above the stage level, are shrubs with vivid trumpet-shaped flowers and a few cactus plants, while at the sides we see the foliage of the encroaching jungle. A tall coconut palm slants upward at one side, its trunk notched for a climber to chop down coconuts for rum-cocos. In the back wall of the verandah are the doors of a line of small cubicle bedrooms which are screened with mosquito-net curtains. For the night scenes they are lighted from within, so that each cubicle appears as a little interior stage, the curtains giving a misty effect to their dim inside lighting. A path which goes down through the rain forest to the highway and the beach, its opening masked by foliage, leads off from one side of the verandah. A canvas hammock is strung from posts on the verandah and there are a few old wicker rockers and rattan lounging chairs at one side.

The Night of the Iguana was presented at the Royale Theatre in New York on December 28, 1961, by Charles Bowden, in association with Violla Rubber. It was directed by Frank Corsaro; the stage setting was designed by Oliver Smith; lighting by Jean Rosenthal; costumes by Noel Taylor; audio effects by Edward Beyer. The cast, in order of appearance, was as follows:

MAXINE FAULK	Bette Davis
PEDRO	James Farentino
PANCHO	Christopher Jones
REVEREND SHANNON	Patrick O'Neal
HANK	Theseus George
HERR FAHRENKOPF	Heinz Hohenwald
FRAU FAHRENKOPF	Lucy Landau
WOLFGANG	Bruce Glover
HILDA	Laryssa Lauret
JUDITH FELLOWES	Patricia Roe
HANNAH JELKES	Margaret Leighton
CHARLOTTE GOODALL	Lane Bradbury
JONATHAN COFFIN (NONNO)	Alan Webb
JAKE LATTA	Louis Guss

Production owned and presented by "The Night of the Iguana" Joint Venture (the joint venture consisting of Charles Bowden and Two Rivers Enterprises, Inc.).

And so, as kinsman met a night,
We talked between the rooms,
Until the moss had reached our lips,
And covered up our names.

—EMILY DICKINSON

As the curtain rises, there are sounds of a party of excited female tourists arriving by bus on the road down the hill below the Costa Verde Hotel. Mrs. Maxine Faulk, the proprietor of the hotel, comes around the turn of the verandah. She is a stout, swarthy woman in her middle forties—affable and rapaciously lusty. She is wearing a pair of Levis and a blouse that is half unbuttoned. She is followed by Pedro, a Mexican of about twenty—slim and attractive. He is an employee in the hotel and also her casual lover. Pedro is stuffing his shirt under the belt of his pants and sweating as if he had been working hard in the sun. Mrs. Faulk looks down the hill and is pleased by the sight of someone coming up from the tourist bus below.

MAXINE [*calling out*]: Shannon! [*A man's voice from below answers: "Hi!"*] Hah! [*Maxine always laughs with a single harsh, loud bark, opening her mouth like a seal expecting a fish to be thrown to it.*] My spies told me that you were back under the border! [*To Pedro.*] Anda, hombre, anda!

[*Maxine's delight expands and vibrates in her as Shannon labors up the hill to the hotel. He does not appear on the jungle path for a minute or two after the shouting between them starts.*]

MAXINE: Hah! My spies told me you went through Saltillo last week with a busload of women—a whole busload of females, all females, hah! How many you laid so far? Hah!

SHANNON [*from below, panting*]: Great Caesar's ghost . . . stop . . . shouting!

MAXINE: No wonder your ass is draggin', hah!

SHANNON: Tell the kid to help me up with this bag.

MAXINE [*shouting directions*]: Pedro! Anda—la maléta. Pancho, no seas flojo! Va y trae el equipaje del señor.

[*Pancho, another young Mexican, comes around the veran-dah and trots down the jungle path. Pedro has climbed up a coconut tree with a machete and is chopping down nuts for rum-cocos.*]

SHANNON [*shouting, below*]: Fred? Hey, Fred!

MAXINE [*with a momentary gravity*]: Fred can't hear you, Shannon. [*She goes over and picks up a coconut, shaking it against her ear to see if it has milk in it.*]

SHANNON [*still below*]: Where is Fred—gone fishing?

[*Maxine lops the end off a coconut with the machete, as Pan-cho trots up to the verandah with Shannon's bag—a beat-up Gladstone covered with travel stickers from all over the world. Then Shannon appears, in a crumpled white linen suit. He is panting, sweating and wild-eyed. About thirty-five, Shannon is "black Irish." His nervous state is terribly apparent; he is a young man who has cracked up before and is going to crack up again—perhaps repeatedly.*]

MAXINE: Well! Lemme look at you!

SHANNON: Don't look at me, get dressed!

MAXINE: Gee, you look like you had it!

SHANNON: You look like you been having it, too. Get dressed!

MAXINE: Hell, I'm dressed. I never dress in September. Don't you know I never dress in September?

SHANNON: Well, just, just—button your shirt up.

MAXINE: How long you been off it, Shannon?

SHANNON: Off what?

MAXINE: The wagon . . .

SHANNON: Hell, I'm dizzy with fever. Hundred and three this morning in Cuernavaca.

MAXINE: Watcha got wrong with you?

SHANNON: Fever . . . fever . . . Where's Fred?

MAXINE: Dead.

SHANNON: Did you say *dead?*

MAXINE: That's what I said. Fred is dead.

SHANNON: How?

MAXINE: Less'n two weeks ago, Fred cut his hand on a fish-hook, it got infected, infection got in his blood stream, and he was dead inside of forty-eight hours. [*To Pancho.*] Vete!

SHANNON: Holy smoke. . . .

MAXINE: I can't quite realize it yet. . . .

SHANNON: You don't seem—inconsolable about it.

MAXINE: Fred was an old man, baby. Ten years older'n me. We hadn't had sex together in. . . .

SHANNON: What's that got to do with it?

MAXINE: Lie down and have a rum-coco.

SHANNON: No, no. I want a cold beer. If I start drinking rum-cocos now I won't stop drinking rum-cocos. So Fred is dead? I looked forward to lying in this hammock and talking to Fred.

MAXINE: Well Fred's not talking now, Shannon. A diabetic gets a blood infection, he goes like that without a decent hospital in less'n a week. [*A bus horn is heard blowing from below.*] Why don't your busload of women come on up here? They're blowing the bus horn down there.

SHANNON: Let 'em blow it, blow it. . . . [*He sways a little.*] I got a fever. [*He goes to the top of the path, divides the flowering bushes and shouts down the hill to the bus.*] Hank! Hank! Get them out of the bus and bring 'em up here! Tell 'em the rates are OK. Tell 'em the. . . . [*His voice gives out, and he stumbles back to the verandah, where he sinks down onto the low steps, panting.*] Absolutely the worst party I've ever been out with in ten years of conducting tours. For God's sake, help me with 'em because I can't go on. I got to rest here a while. [*She gives him a cold beer.*] Thanks. Look and see if they're getting out of the bus. [*She crosses to the masking foliage and separates it to look down the hill.*] Are they getting out of the bus or are they staying in it, the stingy—daughters of—bitches. . . . Schoolteachers at a Baptist Female College in Blowing Rock, Texas. Eleven, eleven of them.

MAXINE: A football squad of old maids.

SHANNON: Yeah, and I'm the football. Are they out of the bus?

MAXINE: One's gotten out—she's going into the bushes.

SHANNON: Well, I've got the ignition key to the bus in my pocket—this pocket—so they can't continue without me unless they walk.

MAXINE: They're still blowin' that horn.

SHANNON: Fantastic. I can't lose this party. Blake Tours has put me on probation because I had a bad party last month that tried to get me sacked and I am now on probation with Blake Tours. If I lose this party I'll be sacked for sure . . . Ah, my God, are they still all in the bus? [*He heaves himself off the steps and staggers back to the path, dividing the foliage to look down it, then shouts.*] Hank! Get them out of the busssss! Bring them up heeee-re!

HANK'S VOICE [*from below*]: They wanta go back in tooooooowwwww-n.

SHANNON: They *can't* go back in toooowwwwn!—Whew—Five years ago this summer I was conducting round-the-world tours for Cook's. Exclusive groups of retired Wall Street financiers. We traveled in fleets of Pierce Arrows and Hispano Suizas.—Are they getting out of the bus?

MAXINE: You're going to pieces, are you?

SHANNON: No! Gone! Gone! [*He rises and shouts down the hill again.*] Hank! Come up here! Come on up here a minute! I wanta talk to you about this situation!—Incredible, fantastic . . . [*He drops back on the steps, his head falling into his hands.*]

MAXINE: They're not getting out of the bus.—Shannon . . . you're not in a nervous condition to cope with this party, Shannon, so let them go and you stay.

SHANNON: You know my situation: I lose this job, what's next? There's nothing lower than Blake Tours, Maxine honey.—Are they getting out of the bus? Are they getting out of it now?

MAXINE: Man's comin' up the hill.

SHANNON: Aw. Hank. You gotta help me with him.

MAXINE: I'll give him a rum-coco.

[*Hank comes grinning onto the verandah.*]

HANK: Shannon, them ladies are not gonna come up here, so you better come on back to the bus.

SHANNON: Fantastic.—I'm not going down to the bus and I've got the ignition key to the bus in my pocket. It's going to stay in my pocket for the next three days.

HANK: You can't get away with that, Shannon. Hell, they'll walk back to town if you don't give up the bus key.

SHANNON: They'd drop like flies from sunstrokes on that road. . . . Fantastic, absolutely fantastic . . . [*Panting and sweating, he drops a hand on Hank's shoulder.*] Hank, I want your co-operation. Can I have it? Because when you're out with a difficult party like this, the tour conductor—me—and the guide—you—have got to stick together to control the situations as they come up against us. It's a test of strength between two men, in this case, and a busload of old wet *hens!* You know that, don't you?

HANK: Well. . . . [*He chuckles.*] There's this kid that's crying on the back seat all the time, and that's what's rucked up the deal. Hell, I don't know if you did or you didn't, but they all think that you did 'cause the kid keeps crying.

SHANNON: *Hank? Look!* I don't care what they think. A tour conducted by T. Lawrence Shannon is in his charge, completely—where to go, when to go, every detail of it. Otherwise I resign. So go on back down there and get them out of that bus before they suffocate in it. Haul them out by force if necessary and herd them up here. Hear me? Don't give me any argument about it. Mrs. Faulk, honey? Give him a menu, give him one of your sample menus to show the ladies. She's got a Chinaman cook here, you won't believe the menu. The cook's from Shanghai, handled the kitchen at an exclusive club there. I got him here for her, and he's a bug, a fanatic about—whew!—continental cuisine . . . can even make beef Strogonoff and thermidor dishes. Mrs. Faulk, honey? Hand him one of those—whew!—one of those fantastic sample menus. [*Maxine chuckles, as if perpetrating a practical joke, as she hands him a sheet of paper.*] Thanks. Now, here. Go on back down there and show them this fantastic menu. Describe the view from the hill, and . . . [*Hank accepts the menu with a chuckling shake of the head.*] And have a cold Carta Blanca and. . . .

HANK: You better go down with me.

SHANNON: I can't leave this verandah for at least forty-eight hours. *What in blazes is this?* A little animated cartoon by Hieronymus Bosch?

[*The German family which is staying at the hotel, the Fahrenkopfs, their daughter and son-in-law, suddenly make a startling, dreamlike entrance upon the scene. They troop around the verandah, then turn down into the jungle path. They are all dressed in the minimal concession to decency and all are pink and gold like baroque cupids in various sizes—Rubensesque, splendidly physical. The bride, Hilda, walks astride a big inflated rubber horse which has an ecstatic smile and great winking eyes. She shouts "Horsey, horsey, giddap!" as she waddles astride it, followed by her Wagnerian-tenor bridegroom, Wolfgang, and her father, Herr Fahrenkopf, a tank manufacturer from Frankfurt. He is carrying a portable short-wave radio, which is tuned in to the crackle and guttural voices of a German broadcast reporting the Battle of Britain. Frau Fahrenkopf, bursting with rich, healthy fat and carrying a basket of food for a picnic at the beach, brings up the rear. They begin to sing a Nazi marching song.*]

SHANNON: Aw—Nazis. How come there's so many of them down here lately?

MAXINE: Mexico's the front door to South America—and the back door to the States, that's why.

SHANNON: Aw, and you're setting yourself up here as a receptionist at both doors, now that Fred's dead? [*Maxine comes over and sits down on him in the hammock.*] Get off my pelvis before you crack it. If you want to crack something, crack some ice for my forehead. [*She removes a chunk of ice from her glass and massages his forehead with it.*]—Ah, God. . . .

MAXINE [*chuckling*]: Ha, so you took the young chick and the old hens are squawking about it, Shannon?

SHANNON: The kid asked for it, no kidding, but she's seventeen—less, a month less'n seventeen. So it's serious, it's very serious, because the kid is not just emotionally precocious, she's a musical prodigy, too.

MAXINE: What's that got to do with it?

SHANNON: Here's what it's got to do with it, she's traveling under the wing, the military escort, of this, this—butch vocal teacher who organizes little community sings in the bus. Ah, God! I'm surprised they're not singing now, they must've already suffocated. Or they'd be singing some morale-boosting number like "She's a Jolly Good Fellow" or "Pop Goes the Weasel."—Oh, God. . . . [*Maxine chuckles up and down the scale.*] And each night after supper, after the complaints about the supper and the check-up on the checks by the math instructor, and the vomiting of the supper by several ladies, who have inspected the kitchen—then the kid, the canary, will give a vocal recital. She opens her mouth and out flies Carrie Jacobs Bond or Ethelbert Nevin. I mean after a day of one indescribable torment after another, such as three blowouts, and a leaking radiator in Tierra Caliente. . . . [*He sits up slowly in the hammock as these recollections gather force.*] And an evening climb up sierras, through torrents of rain, around hairpin turns over gorges and chasms measureless to man, and with a thermos-jug under the driver's seat which the Baptist College ladies think is filled with ice water but which I know is filled with iced tequila—I mean after such a day has finally come to a close, the musical prodigy, Miss Charlotte Goodall, right after supper, before there's a chance to escape, will give a heartbreaking and earsplitting rendition of Carrie Jacobs Bond's "End of a Perfect Day"—with absolutely no humor. . . .

MAXINE: Hah!

SHANNON: Yeah, "Hah!" Last night—no, night before last, the bus burned out its brake linings in Chilpancingo. This town has a hotel . . . this hotel has a piano, which hasn't been tuned since they shot Maximilian. This Texas songbird opens her mouth and out flies "I Love You Truly," and it flies straight at *me,* with *gestures,* all right at *me,* till her chaperone, this Diesel-driven vocal instructor of hers, slams the piano lid down and hauls her out of the mess hall. But as she's hauled out Miss Bird-Girl opens her mouth and out flies, "Larry, Larry, I love you, I love you truly!" That night, when I went to my room, I found that I had a roommate.

MAXINE: The musical prodigy had moved in with you?

SHANNON: The *spook* had moved in with me. In that hot room with one bed, the width of an ironing board and about as hard, the spook was up there on it, sweating, stinking, grinning up at me.

MAXINE: Aw, the spook. [*She chuckles.*] So you've got the spook with you again.

SHANNON: That's right, he's the only passenger that got off the bus with me, honey.

MAXINE: Is he here now?

SHANNON: Not far.

MAXINE: On the verandah?

SHANNON: He might be on the other side of the verandah. Oh, he's around somewhere, but he's like the Sioux Indians in the Wild West fiction, he doesn't attack before sundown, he's an after-sundown shadow. . . .

[*Shannon wriggles out of the hammock as the bus horn gives one last, long protesting blast.*]

MAXINE:

> I have a little shadow
> That goes in and out with me,
> And what can be the use of him
> Is more than I can see.
>
> He's very, very like me,
> From his heels up to his head,
> And he always hops before me
> When I hop into my bed.

SHANNON: That's the truth. He sure hops in the bed with me.

MAXINE: When you're sleeping alone, or . . . ?

SHANNON: I haven't slept in three nights.

MAXINE: Aw, you will tonight, baby.

[*The bus horn sounds again. Shannon rises and squints down the hill at the bus.*]

SHANNON: How long's it take to sweat the faculty of a Baptist Female College out of a bus that's parked in the sun when it's a hundred degrees in the shade?

MAXINE: They're staggering out of it now.

SHANNON: Yeah, I've won *this* round, I reckon. What're they doing down there, can you see?

MAXINE: They're crowding around your pal Hank.

SHANNON: Tearing him to pieces?

MAXINE: One of them's slapped him, he's ducked back into the bus, and she is starting up here.

SHANNON: Oh, Great Caesar's ghost, it's the butch vocal teacher.

MISS FELLOWES [*in a strident voice, from below*]: Shannon! Shannon!

SHANNON: For God's sake, help me with her.

MAXINE: You know I'll help you, baby, but why don't you lay off the young ones and cultivate an interest in normal grown-up women?

MISS FELLOWES [*her voice coming nearer*]: Shannon!

SHANNON [*shouting down the hill*]: Come on up, Miss Fellowes, everything's fixed. [*To Maxine.*] Oh, God, here she comes chargin' up the hill like a bull elephant on a rampage!

[*Miss Fellowes thrashes through the foliage at the top of the jungle path.*]

SHANNON: Miss Fellowes, never do that! Not at high noon in a tropical country in summer. Never charge up a hill like you were leading a troop of cavalry attacking an almost impregnable. . . .

MISS FELLOWES [*panting and furious*]: I don't want advice or instructions, I want the *bus key!*

SHANNON: Mrs. Faulk, this is Miss Judith Fellowes.

MISS FELLOWES: Is this man making a deal with you?

MAXINE: I don't know what you—

MISS FELLOWES: Is this man getting a *kickback* out of you?

MAXINE: Nobody gets any kickback out of me. I turn away more people than—

MISS FELLOWES [*cutting in*]: This isn't the Ambos Mundos. It says in the brochure that in Puerto Barrio we stay at the Ambos Mundos in the heart of the city.

SHANNON: Yes, on the plaza—tell her about the plaza.

MAXINE: What about the plaza?

SHANNON: It's hot, noisy, stinking, swarming with flies. Pariah dogs dying in the—

MISS FELLOWES: How is this place better?

SHANNON: The view from this verandah is equal and I think better than the view from Victoria Peak in Hong Kong, the view from the roof-terrace of the sultan's palace in—

MISS FELLOWES [*cutting in*]: I want the view of a clean bed, a bathroom with plumbing that works, and food that is eatable and digestible and not contaminated by filthy—

SHANNON: *Miss Fellowes!*

MISS FELLOWES: Take your hand off my arm.

SHANNON: Look at this sample menu. The cook is a Chinese imported from Shanghai by *me!* Sent here by *me*, year before last, in nineteen thirty-eight. He was the chef at the Royal Colonial Club in—

MISS FELLOWES [*cutting in*]: You got a telephone here?

MAXINE: Sure, in the office.

MISS FELLOWES: I want to use it—I'll call collect. Where's the office?

MAXINE [*to Pancho*]: Llevala al telefono!

[*With Pancho showing her the way Miss Fellowes stalks off around the verandah to the office. Shannon falls back, sighing desperately, against the verandah wall.*]

MAXINE: Hah!

SHANNON: Why did you have to . . . ?

MAXINE: Huh?

SHANNON: Come out looking like this! For you it's funny but for me it's. . . .

MAXINE: This is how I *look*. What's wrong with how I *look*?

SHANNON: I told you to button your shirt. Are you so proud of your boobs that you won't button your shirt up?—Go in the office and see if she's calling Blake Tours to get me fired.

MAXINE: She better not unless she pays for the call.

[*She goes around the turn of the verandah.*]

[*Miss Hannah Jelkes appears below the verandah steps and stops short as Shannon turns to the wall, pounding his fist against it with a sobbing sound in his throat.*]

HANNAH: Excuse me.

[*Shannon looks down at her, dazed. Hannah is remarkable-looking—ethereal, almost ghostly. She suggests a Gothic cathedral image of a medieval saint, but animated. She could be thirty, she could be forty: she is totally feminine and yet androgynous-looking—almost timeless. She is wearing a cotton print dress and has a bag slung on a strap over her shoulder.*]

HANNAH: Is this the Costa Verde Hotel?

SHANNON [*suddenly pacified by her appearance*]: Yes. Yes, it is.

HANNAH: Are you . . . you're not, the hotel manager, are you?

SHANNON: No. She'll be right back.

HANNAH: Thank you. Do you have any idea if they have two vacancies here? One for myself and one for my grandfather who's waiting in a taxi down there on the road. I didn't want to bring him up the hill—till I'd made sure they have rooms for us first.

SHANNON: Well, there's plenty of room here out-of-season—like now.

HANNAH: Good! Wonderful! I'll get him out of the taxi.

SHANNON: Need any help?

HANNAH: No, thank you. We'll make it all right.

[*She gives him a pleasant nod and goes back off down the path through the rain forest. A coconut plops to the ground; a parrot screams at a distance. Shannon drops into the hammock and stretches out. Then Maxine reappears.*]

SHANNON: How about the call? Did she make a phone call?

MAXINE: She called a judge in Texas—Blowing Rock, Texas. Collect.

SHANNON: She's trying to get me fired and she is also trying to pin on me a rape charge, a charge of statutory rape.

MAXINE: What's "statutory rape"? I've never known what that was.

SHANNON: That's when a man is seduced by a girl under twenty. [*She chuckles.*] It's not funny, Maxine honey.

MAXINE: Why do you want the young ones—or think that you do?

SHANNON: I don't want any, any—regardless of age.

MAXINE: Then why do you take them, Shannon? [*He swallows but does not answer.*]—Huh, Shannon.

SHANNON: People need human contact, Maxine honey.

MAXINE: What size shoe do you wear?

SHANNON: I don't get the point of that question.

MAXINE: These shoes are shot and if I remember correctly, you travel with only one pair. Fred's estate included one good pair of shoes and your feet look about his size.

SHANNON: I loved ole Fred but I don't want to fill his shoes, honey.

[*She has removed Shannon's beat-up, English-made Oxfords.*]

MAXINE: Your socks are shot. Fred's socks would fit you, too, Shannon. [*She opens his collar.*] Aw-aw, I see you got on your gold cross. That's a bad sign, it means you're thinkin' again about goin' back to the Church.

SHANNON: This is my last tour, Maxine. I wrote my old bishop this morning a complete confession and a complete capitulation.

[*She takes a letter from his damp shirt pocket.*]

MAXINE: If this is the letter, baby, you've sweated through it, so the old bugger couldn't read it even if you mailed it to him this time.

[*She has started around the verandah, and goes off as Hank reappears up the hill-path, mopping his face. Shannon's relaxed position in the hammock aggravates Hank sorely.*]

HANK: Will you get your ass out of that hammock?

SHANNON: No, I will not.

HANK: Shannon, git out of that hammock! [*He kicks at Shannon's hips in the hammock.*]

SHANNON: Hank, if you can't function under rough circumstances, you are in the wrong racket, man. I gave you instructions, the instructions were simple. I said get them out of the bus and. . . .

[*Maxine comes back with a kettle of water, a towel and other shaving equipment.*]

HANK: Out of the hammock, Shannon! [*He kicks Shannon again, harder.*]

SHANNON [*warningly*]: That's enough, Hank. A little familiarity goes a long way, but not as far as you're going. [*Maxine starts lathering his face.*] What's this, what are you . . . ?

MAXINE: Haven't you ever had a shave-and-haircut by a lady barber?

HANK: The kid has gone into hysterics.

MAXINE: Hold still, Shannon.

SHANNON: Hank, hysteria is a natural phenomenon, the common denominator of the female nature. It's the big female weapon, and the test of a man is his ability to cope with it, and I can't believe you can't. If I believed that you couldn't, I would not be able—

MAXINE: Hold still!

SHANNON: I'm holding still. [*To Hank.*] No, I wouldn't be able to take you out with me again. So go on back down there and—

HANK: You want me to go back down there and tell them you're getting a shave up here in a hammock?

MAXINE: Tell them that Reverend Larry is going back to the Church so they can go back to the Female College in Texas.

HANK: I want another beer.

MAXINE: Help yourself, piggly-wiggly, the cooler's in my office right around there. [*She points around the corner of the verandah.*]

SHANNON [*as* HANK *goes off*]: It's horrible how you got to bluff and keep bluffing even when hollering "Help!" is all you're up to, Maxine. *You cut me!*

MAXINE: You didn't hold still.

SHANNON: Just trim the beard a little.

MAXINE: I know. Baby, tonight we'll go night-swimming, whether it storms or not.

SHANNON: Ah, God. . . .

MAXINE: The Mexican kids are wonderful night-swimmers. . . . Hah, when I found 'em they were taking the two-hundred-foot dives off the Quebrada, but the Quebrada Hotel kicked 'em out for being overattentive to the lady guests there. That's how I got hold of them.

SHANNON: Maxine, you're bigger than life and twice as unnatural, honey.

MAXINE: No one's bigger than life-size, Shannon, or even ever that big, except maybe Fred. [*She shouts "Fred?" and gets a faint answering echo from an adjoining hill.*] Little Sir Echo is all that answers for him now, Shannon, but. . . . [*She pats some bay rum on his face.*] Dear old Fred was always a mystery to me. He was so patient and tolerant with me that it was insulting to me. A man and a woman have got to challenge each other, y'know what I mean. I mean I hired those diving-boys from the Quebrada six months before Fred died, and did he care? Did he give a damn when I started night-swimming with them? No. He'd go night-

21

fishing, all night, and when I got up the next day, he'd be preparing to go out fishing again, but he just caught the fish and threw them back in the sea.

[*Hank returns and sits drinking his beer on the steps.*]

SHANNON: The mystery of old Fred was simple. He was just cool and decent, that's all the mystery of him. . . . Get your pair of night-swimmers to grab my ladies' luggage out of the bus before the vocal teacher gets off the phone and stops them.

MAXINE [*shouting*]: Pedro! Pancho! Muchachos! Trae las maletas al anejo! Pronto! [*The Mexican boys start down the path. Maxine sits in the hammock beside Shannon.*] You I'll put in Fred's old room, next to me.

SHANNON: You want me in his socks and his shoes and in his room next to *you?* [*He stares at her with a shocked surmise of her intentions toward him, then flops back down in the hammock with an incredulous laugh.*] Oh no, honey. I've just been hanging on till I could get in this hammock on this verandah over the rain forest and the still-water beach, that's all that can put me through this last tour in a condition to go back to my . . . original . . . vocation.

MAXINE: Hah, you still have some rational moments when you face the fact that churchgoers don't go to church to hear atheistical sermons.

SHANNON: Goddamit, I never preached an atheistical sermon in a church in my life, and. . . .

[*Miss Fellowes has charged out of the office and rounds the verandah to bear down on Shannon and Maxine, who jumps up out of the hammock.*]

MISS FELLOWES: I've completed my call, which I made collect to Texas.

[*Maxine shrugs, going by her around the verandah. Miss Fellowes runs across the verandah.*]

SHANNON [*sitting up in the hammock*]: Excuse me, Miss Fellowes, for not getting out of this hammock, but I . . . Miss Fellowes? Please sit down a minute, I want to confess something to you.

MISS FELLOWES: *That* ought to be int'restin'! *What?*

SHANNON: Just that—well, like everyone else, at some point or other in life, my life has cracked up on me.

MISS FELLOWES: How does that compensate *us?*

SHANNON: I don't think I know what you mean by compensate, Miss Fellowes. [*He props himself up and gazes at her with the gentlest bewilderment, calculated to melt a heart of stone.*] I mean I've just confessed to you that I'm at the end of my rope, and you say, "How does that compensate *us?*" Please, Miss Fellowes. Don't make me feel that any adult human being puts personal compensation before the dreadful, bare fact of a man at the end of his rope who still has to try to go on, to continue, as if he'd never been better or stronger in his whole existence. No, don't do that, it would. . . .

MISS FELLOWES: It would *what?*

SHANNON: Shake if not shatter everything left of my faith in essential . . . human . . . *goodness!*

MAXINE [*returning, with a pair of socks*]: Hah!

MISS FELLOWES: Can you sit there, I mean lie there—yeah, I mean lie there . . . ! and talk to me about—

MAXINE: Hah!

MISS FELLOWES: "Essential human goodness"? Why, just plain human decency is beyond your imagination, Shannon, so lie there, lie there and *lie* there, we're *going!*

SHANNON [*rising from the hammock*]: Miss Fellowes, I thought that I was conducting this party, not you.

MISS FELLOWES: You? You just now *admitted* you're incompetent, as well as. . . .

MAXINE: Hah.

SHANNON: Maxine, will you—

MISS FELLOWES [*cutting in with cold, righteous fury*]: *Shannon,* we girls have worked and slaved all year at Baptist Female College for this Mexican tour, and the tour is a cheat!

SHANNON [*to himself*]: Fantastic!

MISS FELLOWES: Yes, *cheat*! You haven't stuck to the schedule and you haven't stuck to the itinerary advertised in the brochure which Blake Tours put out. Now either Blake Tours is cheating us or you are cheating Blake Tours, and I'm putting wheels in motion—I don't care *what* it costs me—I'm. . . .

SHANNON: Oh, Miss Fellowes, isn't it just as plain to you as it is to me that your hysterical insults, which are not at all easy for any born and bred gentleman to accept, are not . . . *motivated, provoked* by . . . anything as *trivial* as the, the . . . the motivations that you're, you're . . . *ascribing* them to? Now can't we talk about the *real, true* cause of. . . .

MISS FELLOWES: Cause of *what*?

[*Charlotte Goodall appears at the top of the hill.*]

SHANNON: —Cause of your *rage* Miss Fellowes, your—

MISS FELLOWES: *Charlotte*! Stay down the hill in the *bus*!

CHARLOTTE: Judy, they're—

MISS FELLOWES: *Obey me! Down!*

[*Charlotte retreats from view like a well-trained dog. Miss Fellowes charges back to Shannon who has gotten out of the hammock. He places a conciliatory hand on her arm.*]

MISS FELLOWES: *Take your hand off my arm!*

MAXINE: Hah!

SHANNON: *Fantastic.* Miss Fellowes, please! No more shouting? Please? Now I really must ask you to let this party of ladies come up here and judge the accommodations for themselves and compare them with what they saw passing through town. Miss Fellowes, there is such a thing as charm and beauty in some places, as much as there's nothing but dull, ugly imitation of highway motels in Texas and—

[*Miss Fellowes charges over to the path to see if Charlotte has obeyed her. Shannon follows, still propitiatory. Maxine says* "Hah," *but she gives him an affectionate little pat as he goes by her. He pushes her hand away as he continues his appeal to Miss Fellowes.*]

MISS FELLOWES: I've taken a look at those rooms and they'd make a room at the "Y" look like a suite at the Ritz.

SHANNON: Miss Fellowes, I am employed by Blake Tours and so I'm not in a position to tell you quite frankly what mistakes they've made in their advertising brochure. They just don't know Mexico. I do. I know it as well as I know five out of all six continents on the—

MISS FELLOWES: *Continent! Mexico?* You never even studied geography if you—

SHANNON: My degree from Sewanee is *Doctor* of *Divinity,* but for the past ten years geography's been my *specialty,* Miss Fellowes, honey! Name any tourist agency I haven't worked for! You couldn't! I'm only, now, with Blake Tours because I—

MISS FELLOWES: Because you *what?* Couldn't keep your hands off innocent, underage girls in your—

SHANNON: Now, Miss Fellowes. . . . [*He touches her arm again.*]

MISS FELLOWES: Take your hand off my arm!

SHANNON: For days I've known you were furious and unhappy, but—

MISS FELLOWES: *Oh!* You think it's just *me* that's unhappy! Hauled in that stifling bus over the byways, off the highways, shook up and bumped up so you could get your rake-off, is that what you—

SHANNON: What I know is, all I know is, that you are the *leader* of the *insurrection!*

MISS FELLOWES: All of the girls in this party have dysentery!

SHANNON: That you can't hold me to blame for.

MISS FELLOWES: I *do* hold you to blame for it.

SHANNON: Before we entered Mexico, at New Laredo, Texas, I called you ladies together in the depot on the Texas side of the border and I passed out mimeographed sheets of instructions on what to eat and what *not* to eat, what to drink, what *not* to drink in the—

MISS FELLOWES: It's not *what* we ate but *where* we ate that gave us dysentery!

SHANNON [*shaking his head like a metronome*]: It is not dysentery.

MISS FELLOWES: The result of eating in places that would be condemned by the Board of Health in—

SHANNON: Now wait a minute—

MISS FELLOWES: For disregarding all rules of sanitation.

SHANNON: It is not dysentery, it is not amoebic, it's nothing at all but—

MAXINE: Montezuma's Revenge! That's what we call it.

SHANNON: I even passed out pills. I passed out bottles of Enteroviaform because I knew that some of you ladies would rather be victims of Montezuma's Revenge than spend cinco centavos on bottled water in stations.

MISS FELLOWES: You sold those pills at a profit of fifty cents per bottle.

MAXINE: Hah-hah! [*She knocks off the end of a coconut with the machete, preparing a rum-coco.*]

SHANNON: Now fun is fun, Miss Fellowes, but an accusation like that—

MISS FELLOWES: I *priced* them in *pharmacies*, because I suspected that—

SHANNON: Miss Fellowes, I am a gentleman, and as a gentleman I can't be insulted like this. I mean I can't accept insults of that kind even from a member of a tour that I am conducting. And, Miss Fellowes, I think you might also remember, you might try to remember, that you're speaking to an ordained minister of the Church.

MISS FELLOWES: *De*-frocked! But still trying to pass himself off as a minister!

MAXINE: How about a rum-coco? We give a complimentary rum-coco to all our guests here. [*Her offer is apparently unheard. She shrugs and drinks the rum-coco herself.*]

SHANNON: —Miss Fellowes? In every party there is always one individual that's discontented, that is not satisfied with all I do to make the tour more . . . unique—to make it different from the ordinary, to give it a personal thing, the Shannon touch.

MISS FELLOWES: The gyp touch, the touch of a defrocked minister.

SHANNON: Miss Fellowes, don't, don't, don't . . . do what . . . you're doing! [*He is on the verge of hysteria, he makes some incoherent sounds, gesticulates with clenched fists, then stumbles wildly across the verandah and leans panting for breath against a post.*] Don't! Break! *Human! Pride!*

VOICE FROM DOWN THE HILL [*a very Texan accent*]: Judy? They're taking our luggage!

MISS FELLOWES [*shouting down the hill*]: Girls! Girls! Don't let those boys touch your luggage. Don't let them bring your luggage in this dump!

GIRL'S VOICE [*from below*]: Judy! We can't stop them!

MAXINE: Those kids don't understand English.

MISS FELLOWES [*wild with rage*]: Will you please tell those boys to take that luggage back down to the bus? [*She calls to the party below again.*] Girls! Hold onto your luggage, don't let them take it away! We're going to drive back to A-cap-ul-co! *You hear?*

GIRL'S VOICE: Judy, they want a swim, first!

MISS FELLOWES: I'll be right back. [*She rushes off, shouting at the Mexican boys.*] You! Boys! Muchachos! *You carry that luggage back down!*

[*The voices continue, fading. Shannon moves brokenly across the verandah. Maxine shakes her head.*]

MAXINE: Shannon, give 'em the bus key and let 'em go.

SHANNON: And me do what?

MAXINE: Stay here.

SHANNON: In Fred's old bedroom—yeah, in Fred's old bedroom.

MAXINE: You could do worse.

SHANNON: Could I? Well, then, I'll do worse, I'll . . . do worse.

MAXINE: Aw now, baby.

SHANNON: If I could do worse, I'll do worse. . . . [*He grips the section of railing by the verandah steps and stares with wide, lost eyes. His chest heaves like a spent runner's and he is bathed in sweat.*]

MAXINE: Give me that ignition key. I'll take it down to the driver while you bathe and rest and have a rum-coco, baby.

[*Shannon simply shakes his head slightly. Harsh bird cries sound in the rain forest. Voices are heard on the path.*]

HANNAH: Nonno, you've lost your sunglasses.

NONNO: No. Took them off. No sun.

[*Hannah appears at the top of the path, pushing her grandfather, Nonno, in a wheelchair. He is a very old man but has a powerful voice for his age and always seems to be shouting something of importance. Nonno is a poet and a showman. There is a good kind of pride and he has it, carrying it like a banner wherever he goes. He is immaculately dressed—a linen suit, white as his thick poet's hair; a black string tie; and he is holding a black cane with a gold crook.*]

NONNO: Which way is the sea?

HANNAH: Right down below the hill, Nonno. [*He turns in the wheelchair and raises a hand to shield his eyes.*] We can't see it from here. [*The old man is deaf, and she shouts to make him hear.*]

NONNO: I can feel it and smell it. [*A murmur of wind sweeps through the rain forest.*] It's the cradle of life. [*He is shouting, too.*] Life began in the sea.

MAXINE: These two with your party?

SHANNON: No.

MAXINE: They look like a pair of loonies.

SHANNON: Shut up.

[*Shannon looks at Hannah and Nonno steadily, with a relief of tension almost like that of someone going under hypnosis. The old man still squints down the path, blindly, but Hannah is facing the verandah with a proud person's hope of acceptance when it is desperately needed.*]

HANNAH: How do you do.

MAXINE: Hello.

HANNAH: Have you ever tried pushing a gentleman in a wheel-chair uphill through a rain forest?

MAXINE: Nope, and I wouldn't even try it *downhill.*

HANNAH: Well, now that we've made it, I don't regret the ef-fort. What a view for a painter! [*She looks about her, panting, dig-ging into her shoulder-bag for a handkerchief, aware that her face is flushed and sweating.*] They told me in town that this was the ideal place for a painter, and they weren't—*whew*—exaggerating!

SHANNON: You've got a scratch on your forehead.

HANNAH: Oh, is that what I felt.

SHANNON: Better put iodine on it.

HANNAH: Yes, I'll attend to that—*whew*—later, thank you.

MAXINE: Anything I can do for you?

HANNAH: I'm looking for the manager of the hotel.

MAXINE: Me—speaking.

HANNAH: Oh, *you're* the manager, *good!* How do you do, I'm Hannah Jelkes, Mrs. . . .

MAXINE: Faulk, Maxine Faulk. What can I do for you folks? [*Her tone indicates no desire to do anything for them.*]

HANNAH: [*turning quickly to her grandfather*]: Nonno, the manager is a *lady* from the *States.*

[*Nonno lifts a branch of wild orchids from his lap, ceremonially, with the instinctive gallantry of his kind.*]

NONNO: [*shouting*]: Give the lady these—botanical curiosities!— you picked on the way up.

HANNAH: I believe they're wild orchids, isn't that what they are?

SHANNON: Laelia tibicina.

HANNAH: Oh!

NONNO: But tell her, Hannah, tell her to keep them in the ice- box till after dark, they draw bees in the sun! [*He rubs a sting on his chin with a rueful chuckle.*]

MAXINE: Are you all looking for rooms here?

HANNAH: Yes, we are, but we've come without reservations.

MAXINE: Well, honey, the Costa Verde is closed in September— except for a few special guests, so. . . .

SHANNON: They're special guests, for God's sake.

MAXINE: I thought you said they didn't come with your party.

HANNAH: Please let us be special guests.

MAXINE: *Watch out!*

[*Nonno has started struggling out of the wheelchair. Shannon rushes over to keep him from falling. Hannah has started toward him, too, then seeing that Shannon has caught him, she turns back to Maxine.*]

HANNAH: In twenty-five years of travel this is the first time we've ever arrived at a place without advance reservations.

MAXINE: Honey, that old man ought to be in a hospital.

HANNAH: Oh, no, no, he just sprained his ankle a little in Taxco this morning. He just needs a good night's rest, he'll be on his feet tomorrow. His recuperative powers are absolutely amazing for someone who is ninety-seven years *young.*

SHANNON: Easy, Grampa. Hang on. [*He is supporting the old man up to the verandah.*] Two steps. One! Two! Now you've made it, Grampa.

[*Nonno keeps chuckling breathlessly as Shannon gets him onto the verandah and into a wicker rocker.*]

HANNAH [*breaking in quickly*]: I can't tell you how much I appreciate your taking us in here now. It's—providential.

MAXINE: Well, I can't send that old man back down the hill right now—but like I told you the Costa Verde's practically closed in September. I just take in a few folks as a special accommodation and we operate on a special basis this month.

NONNO [*cutting in abruptly and loudly*]: Hannah, tell the lady that my perambulator is temporary. I will soon be ready to crawl and then to toddle and before long I will be leaping around here like an—old—mountain—goat, ha-ha-ha-ha. . . .

HANNAH: Yes, I explained that, Grandfather.

NONNO: I don't like being on wheels.

HANNAH: Yes, my grandfather feels that the decline of the Western world began with the invention of the wheel. [*She laughs heartily, but Maxine's look is unresponsive.*]

NONNO: And tell the manager . . . the, uh, lady . . . that I know some hotels don't want to take dogs, cats or monkeys and some don't even solicit the patronage of infants in their late nineties who arrive in perambulators with flowers instead of rattles . . . [*He chuckles with a sort of fearful, slightly mad quality. Hannah perhaps has the impulse to clap a hand over his mouth at this moment but must stand there smiling and smiling and smiling.*] . . . and a brandy flask instead of a teething ring, but tell her that these, uh, concessions to man's seventh age are only temporary, and. . . .

HANNAH: Nonno, I told her the wheelchair's because of a sprained ankle, Nonno!

SHANNON [*to himself*]: Fantastic.

NONNO: And after my siesta, I'll wheel it back down the hill, I'll kick it back down the hill, right into the sea, and tell her. . . .

HANNAH: Yes? What, Nonno? [*She has stopped smiling now. Her tone and her look are frankly desperate.*] What shall I tell her now, Nonno?

NONNO: Tell her that if she'll forgive my disgraceful longevity and this . . . temporary decrepitude . . . I will present her with the last signed . . . compitty [*he means "copy"*] of my first volume of verse, published in . . . when, Hannah?

HANNAH [*hopelessly*]: The day that President Ulysses S. Grant was inaugurated, Nonno.

NONNO: *Morning Trumpet!* Where is it—you have it, give it to her right now.

HANNAH: Later, a little later! [*Then she turns to Maxine and Shannon.*] My grandfather is the poet Jonathan Coffin. He is ninety-seven years *young* and will be ninety-eight years *young* the fifth of next month, October.

MAXINE: Old folks are remarkable, yep. The office phone's ringing—excuse me, I'll be right back. [*She goes around the verandah.*]

NONNO: Did I talk too much?

HANNAH [*quietly, to Shannon*]: I'm afraid that he did. I don't think she's going to take us.

SHANNON: She'll take you. Don't worry about it.

HANNAH: Nobody would take us in town, and if we don't get in here, I would have to wheel him back down through the rain forest, and then *what,* then *where?* There would just be the road, and no direction to move in, except out to sea—and I doubt that we could make it divide before us.

SHANNON: That won't be necessary. I have a little influence with the patrona.

HANNAH: Oh, then, do use it, please. Her eyes said *no* in big blue capital letters.

[*Shannon pours some water from a pitcher on the verandah and hands it to the old man.*]

NONNO: What is this—libation?

SHANNON: Some ice water, Grampa.

HANNAH: Oh, that's kind of you. Thank you. I'd better give him a couple of salt tablets to wash down with it. [*Briskly she removes a bottle from her shoulder-bag.*] Won't you have some? I see you're perspiring, too. You have to be careful not to become dehydrated in the hot seasons under the Tropic of Cancer.

SHANNON [*pouring another glass of water*]: Are you a little *financially* dehydrated, too?

HANNAH: That's right. Bone dry, and I think the patrona suspects it. It's a logical assumption, since I pushed him up here myself, and the patrona has the look of a very logical woman. I am sure she knows that we couldn't afford to hire the taxi driver to help us up here.

MAXINE [*calling from the back*]: Pancho?

HANNAH: A woman's practicality when she's managing something is harder than a man's for another woman to cope with, so if you have influence with her, please do use it. Please try to convince her that my grandfather will be on his feet tomorrow, if not tonight, and with any luck whatsoever, the money situation will be solved just as quickly. Oh, here she comes back, do help us!

[*Involuntarily Hannah seizes hold of Shannon's wrist as Maxine stalks back onto the verandah, still shouting for Pancho. The Mexican boy reappears, sucking a juicy peeled mango—its juice running down his chin onto his throat.*]

MAXINE: Pancho, run down to the beach and tell Herr Fahrenkopf that the German Embassy's waiting on the phone for him. [*Pancho stares at her blankly until she repeats the order in Spanish.*] Dile a Herr Fahrenkopf que la embajada alemana lo llama al telefono. Corre, corre! [*Pancho starts indolently down the path, still sucking noisily on the mango.*] I said *run!* Corre, corre! [*He goes into a leisurely loping pace and disappears through the foliage.*]

HANNAH: What graceful people they are!

MAXINE: Yeah, they're graceful like cats, and just as dependable, too.

HANNAH: Shall we, uh, . . . *register* now?

MAXINE: You all can register later but I'll have to collect six dollars from you first if you want to put your names in the pot for supper. That's how I've got to operate here out of season.

HANNAH: Six? Dollars?

MAXINE: Yeah, three each. In season we operate on the continental plan but out of season like this we change to the modified American plan.

HANNAH: Oh, what is the, uh . . . modification of it? [*She gives Shannon a quick glance of appeal as she stalls for time, but his attention has turned inward as the bus horn blows down the hill.*]

MAXINE: Just two meals are included instead of all three.

HANNAH [*moving closer to Shannon and raising her voice*]: Breakfast and dinner?

MAXINE: A continental breakfast and a cold lunch.

SHANNON [*aside*]: Yeah, very cold—cracked ice—if you crack it yourself.

HANNAH [*reflectively*]: Not dinner.

MAXINE: No! Not dinner.

HANNAH: Oh, I see, uh, but . . . we, uh, operate on a special basis ourselves. I'd better explain it to you.

MAXINE: How do you mean "operate"—on what "basis"?

HANNAH: Here's our card. I think you may have heard of us. [*She presents the card to Maxine.*] We've had a good many write-ups. My grandfather is the oldest living and practicing poet. *And* he gives recitations. I . . . paint . . . water colors and I'm a "quick sketch artist." We travel together. We pay our way as we go by my grandfather's recitations and the sale of my water colors and quick character sketches in charcoal or pastel.

SHANNON [*to himself*]: I have fever.

HANNAH: I usually pass among the tables at lunch and dinner in a hotel. I wear an artist's smock—picturesquely dabbed with paint—wide Byronic collar and flowing silk tie. I don't push myself on people. I just display my work and smile at them sweetly and if they invite me to do so sit down to make a quick character sketch in pastel or charcoal. If not? Smile sweetly and go on.

SHANNON: What does Grandpa do?

HANNAH: We pass among the tables together slowly. I introduce him as the world's oldest living and practicing poet. If invited, he gives a recitation of a poem. Unfortunately all of his poems were written a long time ago. But do you know, he has started a new poem? For the first time in twenty years he's started another poem!

SHANNON: Hasn't finished it yet?

HANNAH: He still has inspiration, but his power of concentration has weakened a little, of course.

MAXINE: Right now he's not concentrating.

SHANNON: Grandpa's catchin' forty winks. Grampa? Let's hit the sack.

37

MAXINE: Now wait a minute. I'm going to call a taxi for these folks to take them back to town.

HANNAH: Please don't do that. We tried every hotel in town and they wouldn't take us. I'm afraid I have to place myself at your . . . mercy.

[*With infinite gentleness Shannon has roused the old man and is leading him into one of the cubicles back of the verandah. Distant cries of bathers are heard from the beach. The afternoon light is fading very fast now as the sun has dropped behind an island hilltop out to sea.*]

MAXINE: Looks like you're in for one night. Just one.

HANNAH: Thank you.

MAXINE: The old man's in number 4. You take 3. Where's your luggage—no luggage?

HANNAH: I hid it behind some palmettos at the foot of the path.

SHANNON [*shouting to Pancho*]: Bring up her luggage. Tu, flojo . . . las maletas . . . baja las palmas. Vamos! [*The Mexican boys rush down the path.*] Maxine honey, would you cash a post-dated check for me?

MAXINE [*shrewdly*]: Yeah—mañana, maybe.

SHANNON: Thanks—generosity is the cornerstone of your nature.

[*Maxine utters her one-note bark of a laugh as she marches around the corner of the verandah.*]

HANNAH: I'm dreadfully afraid my grandfather had a slight stroke in those high passes through the sierras. [*She says this with the coolness of someone saying that it may rain before nightfall.*

An instant later, a long, long sigh of wind sweeps the hillside. The bathers are heard shouting below.]

SHANNON: Very old people get these little "cerebral accidents," as they call them. They're not regular strokes, they're just little cerebral . . . incidents. The symptoms clear up so quickly that sometimes the old people don't even know they've had them.

[*They exchange this quiet talk without looking at each other. The Mexican boys crash back through the bushes at the top of the path, bearing some pieces of ancient luggage fantastically plastered with hotel and travel stickers indicating a vast range of wandering. The boys deposit the luggage near the steps.*]

SHANNON: How many times have you been around the world?

HANNAH: Almost as many times as the world's been around the sun, and I feel as if I had gone the whole way on foot.

SHANNON [*picking up her luggage*]: What's your cell number?

HANNAH [*smiling faintly*]: I believe she said it was cell number 3.

SHANNON: She probably gave you the one with the leaky roof. [*He carries the bags into the cubicle. Maxine is visible to the audience only as she appears outside the door to her office on the wing of the verandah.*] But you won't find out till it rains and then it'll be too late to do much about it but swim out of it. [*Hannah laughs wanly. Her fatigue is now very plain. Shannon comes back out with her luggage.*] Yep, she gave you the one with the leaky roof so you take mine and. . . .

HANNAH: Oh, no, no, Mr. Shannon, I'll find a dry spot if it rains.

MAXINE [*from around the corner of the verandah*]: Shannon!

39

[*A bit of pantomime occurs between Hannah and Shannon. He wants to put her luggage in cubicle number 5. She catches hold of his arm, indicating by gesture toward the back that it is necessary to avoid displeasing the proprietor. Maxine shouts his name louder. Shannon surrenders to Hannah's pleading and puts her luggage back in the leaky cubicle number 3.*]

HANNAH: Thank you so much, Mr. Shannon. [*She disappears behind the mosquito netting. Maxine advances to the verandah angle as Shannon starts toward his own cubicle.*]

MAXINE [*mimicking Hannah's voice*]: "Thank you so much, Mr. Shannon."

SHANNON: Don't be bitchy. Some people say thank you sincerely. [*He goes past her and down the steps from the end of the verandah.*] I'm going down for a swim now.

MAXINE: The water's blood temperature this time of day.

SHANNON: Yeah, well, I have a fever so it'll seem cooler to me. [*He crosses rapidly to the jungle path leading to the beach.*]

MAXINE [*following him*]: Wait for me, I'll. . . .

[*She means she will go down with him, but he ignores her call and disappears into the foliage. Maxine shrugs angrily and goes back onto the verandah. She faces out, gripping the railing tightly and glaring into the blaze of the sun as if it were a personal enemy. Then the ocean breathes a long cooling breath up the hill, as Nonno's voice is heard from his cubicle*]

NONNO:

> How calmly does the orange branch
> Observe the sky begin to blanch,
> Without a cry, without a prayer,
> With no expression of despair. . . .

[*And from a beach cantina in the distance a marimba band is heard playing a popular song of that summer of 1940,* "*Palabras de Mujer*"—*which means* "*Words of Women.*"]

SLOW DIM OUT AND SLOW CURTAIN

Several hours later: near sunset.

The scene is bathed in a deep golden, almost coppery light; the heavy tropical foliage gleams with wetness from a recent rain.

Maxine comes around the turn of the verandah. To the formalities of evening she has made the concession of changing from Levis to clean white cotton pants, and from a blue work shirt to a pink one. She is about to set up the folding cardtables for the evening meal which is served on the verandah. All the while she is talking, she is setting up tables, etc.

MAXINE: Miss Jelkes?

[*Hannah lifts the mosquito net over the door of cubicle number 3.*]

HANNAH: Yes, Mrs. Faulk?

MAXINE: Can I speak to you while I set up these tables for supper?

HANNAH: Of course, you may. I wanted to speak to you, too. [*She comes out. She is now wearing her artist's smock.*]

MAXINE: Good.

HANNAH: I just wanted to ask you if there's a tub-bath Grandfather could use. A shower is fine for me—I prefer a shower to a tub—but for my grandfather there is some danger of falling down in a shower and at his age, although he says he is made out of India rubber, a broken hipbone would be a very serious matter, so I. . . .

MAXINE: What I wanted to say is I called up the Casa de Huéspedes about you and your Grampa, and I can get you in there.

HANNAH: Oh, but we don't want to *move*!

MAXINE: The Costa Verde isn't the right place for you. Y'see, we cater to folks that like to rough it a little, and—well, frankly, we cater to younger people.

[*Hannah has started unfolding a cardtable.*]

HANNAH: Oh yes . . . uh . . . well . . . the, uh, Casa de Hués-pedes, that means a, uh, sort of a rooming house, Mrs. Faulk?

MAXINE: Boardinghouse. They feed you, they'll even feed you on credit.

HANNAH: Where is it located?

MAXINE: It has a central location. You could get a doctor there quick if the old man took sick on you. You got to think about that.

HANNAH: Yes, I—[*She nods gravely, more to herself than Maxine.*]—I *have* thought about that, but. . . .

MAXINE: What are you doing?

HANNAH: Making myself useful.

MAXINE: Don't do that. I don't accept help from guests here.

[*Hannah hesitates, but goes on setting the tables.*]

HANNAH: Oh, please, let me. Knife and fork on one side, spoon on the . . . ? [*Her voice dies out.*]

MAXINE: Just put the plates on the napkins so they don't blow away.

HANNAH: Yes, it is getting breezy on the verandah. [*She continues setting the table.*]

MAXINE: Hurricane winds are already hitting up coast.

43

HANNAH: We've been through several typhoons in the Orient. Sometimes *outside* disturbances like that are an almost welcome distraction from *inside* disturbances, aren't they? [*This is said almost to herself. She finishes putting the plates on the paper napkins.*] When do you want us to leave here, Mrs. Faulk?

MAXINE: The boys'll move you in my station wagon tomorrow—no charge for the service.

HANNAH: That is very kind of you. [*Maxine starts away.*] Mrs. Faulk?

MAXINE [*turning back to her with obvious reluctance*]: Huh?

HANNAH: Do you know jade?

MAXINE: Jade?

HANNAH: Yes.

MAXINE: Why?

HANNAH: I have a small but interesting collection of jade pieces. I asked if you know jade because in jade it's the craftsmanship, the carving of the jade, that's most important about it. [*She has removed a jade ornament from her blouse.*] This one, for instance—a miracle of carving. Tiny as it is, it has two figures carved on it—the legendary Prince Ahk and Princess Angh, and a heron flying above them. The artist that carved it probably received for this miraculously delicate workmanship, well, I would say perhaps the price of a month's supply of rice for his family, but the merchant who employed him sold it, I would guess, for at least three hundred pounds sterling to an English lady who got tired of it and gave it to me, perhaps because I painted her not as she was at that time but as I could see she must have looked in her youth. Can you see the carving?

MAXINE: Yeah, honey, but I'm not operating a hock shop here, I'm trying to run a hotel.

HANNAH: I know, but couldn't you just accept it as security for a few days' stay here?

MAXINE: You're completely broke, are you?

HANNAH: Yes, we are—completely.

MAXINE: You say that like you're proud of it.

HANNAH: I'm not proud of it or ashamed of it either. It just happens to be what's happened to us, which has never happened before in all our travels.

MAXINE [grudgingly]: You're telling the truth, I reckon, but I told you the truth, too, when I told you, when you came here, that I had just lost my husband and he'd left me in such a financial hole that if living didn't mean more to me than money, I'd might as well have been dropped in the ocean with him.

HANNAH: Ocean?

MAXINE [peacefully philosophical about it]: I carried out his burial instructions exactly. Yep, my husband, Fred Faulk, was the greatest game fisherman on the West Coast of Mexico—he'd racked up unbeatable records in sailfish, tarpon, kingfish, barracuda—and on his deathbed, last week, he requested to be dropped in the sea, yeah, right out there in that bay, not even sewed up in canvas, just in his fisherman outfit. So now old Freddie the Fisherman is feeding the fish—fishes' revenge on old Freddie. How about that, I ask you?

HANNAH [regarding Maxine sharply]: I doubt that he regrets it.

MAXINE: I do. It gives me the shivers.

[*She is distracted by the German party singing a marching song on the path up from the beach. Shannon appears at the top of the path, a wet beachrobe clinging to him. Maxine's whole concentration shifts abruptly to him. She freezes and blazes with it like an exposed power line. For a moment the "hot light" is concentrated on her tense, furious figure. Hannah provides a visual counterpoint. She clenches her eyes shut for a moment, and when they open, it is on a look of stoical despair of the refuge she has unsuccessfully fought for. Then Shannon approaches the verandah and the scene is his.*]

SHANNON: Here they come up, your conquerors of the world, Maxine honey, singing "Horst Wessel." [*He chuckles fiercely, and starts toward the verandah steps.*]

MAXINE: Shannon, wash that sand off you before you come on the verandah.

[*The Germans are heard singing the "Horst Wessel" marching song. Soon they appear, trooping up from the beach like an animated canvas by Rubens. They are all nearly nude, pinked and bronzed by the sun. The women have decked themselves with garlands of pale green seaweed, glistening wet, and the Munich-opera bridegroom is blowing on a great conch shell. His father-in-law, the tank manufacturer, has his portable radio, which is still transmitting a short-wave broadcast about the Battle of Britain, now at its climax.*]

HILDA [*capering, astride her rubber horse*]: Horsey, horsey, horsey!

HERR FAHRENKOPF [*ecstatically*]: London is burning, the heart of London's on fire! [*Wolfgang turns a handspring onto the verandah and walks on his hands a few paces, then tumbles over with a great whoop. Maxine laughs delightedly with the Germans.*] Beer, beer, beer!

FRAU FAHRENKOPF: Tonight champagne!

[*The euphoric horseplay and shouting continue as they gambol around the turn of the verandah. Shannon has come onto the porch. Maxine's laughter dies out a little sadly, with envy.*]

SHANNON: You're turning this place into the Mexican Berchtesgaden, Maxine honey?

MAXINE: I told you to wash that sand off. [*Shouts for beer from the Germans draw her around the verandah corner.*]

HANNAH: Mr. Shannon, do you happen to know the Casa de Huéspedes, or anything about it, I mean? [*Shannon stares at her somewhat blankly.*] We are, uh, thinking of . . . *moving* there tomorrow. Do you, uh, recommend it?

SHANNON: I recommend it along with the Black Hole of Calcutta and the Siberian salt mines.

HANNAH [*nodding reflectively*]: I suspected as much. Mr. Shannon, in your touring party, do you think there might be anyone interested in my water colors? Or in my character sketches?

SHANNON: I doubt it. I doubt that they're corny enough to please my ladies. *Oh-oh! Great Caesar's ghost. . . .*

[*This exclamation is prompted by the shrill, approaching call of his name. Charlotte appears from the rear, coming from the hotel annex, and rushes like a teen-age Medea toward the verandah. Shannon ducks into his cubicle, slamming the door so quickly that a corner of the mosquito netting is caught and sticks out, flirtatiously. Charlotte rushes onto the verandah.*]

CHARLOTTE: *Larry!*

HANNAH: Are you looking for someone, dear?

CHARLOTTE: Yeah, the man conducting our tour, Larry Shannon.

HANNAH: Oh, Mr. Shannon. I think he went down to the beach.

CHARLOTTE: I just now saw him coming up from the beach. [*She is tense and trembling, and her eyes keep darting up and down the verandah.*]

HANNAH: Oh. Well. . . . But. . . .

CHARLOTTE: Larry? Larry! [*Her shouts startle the rain-forest birds into a clamorous moment.*]

HANNAH: Would you like to leave a message for him, dear?

CHARLOTTE: No. I'm staying right here till he comes out of wherever he's hiding.

HANNAH: Why don't you just sit down, dear. I'm an artist, a painter. I was just sorting out my water colors and sketches in this portfolio, and look what I've come across. [*She selects a sketch and holds it up.*]

SHANNON [*from inside his cubicle*]: Oh, God!

CHARLOTTE [*darting to the cubicle*]: Larry, let me in there!

[*She beats on the door of the cubicle as Herr Fahrenkopf comes around the verandah with his portable radio. He is bug-eyed with excitement over the news broadcast in German.*]

HANNAH: Guten abend.

[*Herr Fahrenkopf jerks his head with a toothy grin, raising a hand for silence. Hannah nods agreeably and approaches him with her portfolio of drawings. He maintains the grin as she displays one picture after another. Hannah is uncertain whether the*

*grin is for the pictures or the news broadcast. He stares at the
pictures, jerking his head from time to time. It is rather like the
pantomine of showing lantern slides.*]

CHARLOTTE [*suddenly crying out again*]: Larry, open this door
and let me in! I know you're in there, Larry!

HERR FAHRENKOPF: Silence, please, for one moment! This is
a recording of Der Führer addressing the Reichstag just . . . [*He
glances at his wrist watch.*] . . . eight hours ago, today, transmit-
ted by Deutsches Nachrichtenbüro to Mexico City. Please! Quiet,
bitte!

[*A human voice like a mad dog's bark emerges from the static
momentarily. Charlotte goes on pounding on Shannon's door.
Hannah suggests in pantomime that they go to the back verandah, but Herr Fahrenkopf despairs of hearing the broadcast.
As he rises to leave, the light catches his polished glasses so that
he appears for a moment to have electric light bulbs in his forehead. Then he ducks his head in a genial little bow and goes out
beyond the verandah, where he performs some muscle-flexing
movements of a formalized nature, like the preliminary stances
of Japanese Suma wrestlers.*]

HANNAH: May I show you my work on the other verandah?

[*Hannah had started to follow Herr Fahrenkopf with her portfolio, but the sketches fall out, and she stops to gather them
from the floor with the sad, preoccupied air of a lonely child
picking flowers.*]

[*Shannon's head slowly, furtively, appears through the window of his cubicle. He draws quickly back as Charlotte darts
that way, stepping on Hannah's spilt sketches. Hannah utters
a soft cry of protest, which is drowned by Charlotte's renewed
clamor.*]

CHARLOTTE: Larry, Larry, Judy's looking for me. Let me come in, Larry, before she finds me here!

SHANNON: You can't come in. Stop shouting and I'll come out.

CHARLOTTE: All right, come out.

SHANNON: Stand back from the door so I *can*.

[*She moves a little aside and he emerges from his cubicle like a man entering a place of execution. He leans against the wall, mopping the sweat off his face with a handkerchief.*]

SHANNON: How does Miss Fellowes know what happened that night? Did you tell her?

CHARLOTTE: I didn't tell her, she guessed.

SHANNON: Guessing isn't knowing. If she is just guessing, that means she doesn't know—I mean if you're not lying, if you didn't tell her.

[*Hannah has finished picking up her drawings and moves quietly over to the far side of the verandah.*]

CHARLOTTE: Don't talk to me like that.

SHANNON: Don't complicate my life now, please, for God's sake, don't complicate my life now.

CHARLOTTE: Why have you changed like this?

SHANNON: I have a fever. Don't complicate my . . . fever.

CHARLOTTE: You act like you hated me now.

SHANNON: You're going to get me kicked out of Blake Tours, Charlotte.

CHARLOTTE: Judy is, not me.

SHANNON: Why did you sing "I Love You Truly" at me?

CHARLOTTE: Because I do love you truly!

SHANNON: Honey girl, don't you know that nothing worse could happen to a girl in your, your . . . unstable condition . . . than to get emotionally mixed up with a man in my unstable condition, huh?

CHARLOTTE: No, no, no, I—

SHANNON [*cutting through*]: Two unstable conditions can set a whole world on fire, can blow it up, past repair, and that is just as true between two people as it's true between. . . .

CHARLOTTE: All I know is you've got to marry me, Larry, after what happened between us in Mexico City!

SHANNON: A man in my condition can't marry, it isn't decent or legal. He's lucky if he can even hold onto his job. [*He keeps catching hold of her hands and plucking them off his shoulders.*] I'm almost out of my mind, can't you see that, honey?

CHARLOTTE: I don't believe you don't love me.

SHANNON: Honey, it's almost impossible for anybody to believe they're not loved by someone they believe they love, but, honey, I love *nobody*. I'm like that, it isn't my fault. When I brought you home that night I told you good night in the hall, just kissed you on the cheek like the little girl that you are, but the instant I opened my door, you rushed into my room and I couldn't get you out of it, not even when I, oh God, tried to scare you out of it by, oh God, don't you remember?

[*Miss Fellowes' voice is heard from back of the hotel calling, "Charlotte!"*]

CHARLOTTE: Yes, I remember that after making love to me, you hit me, Larry, you struck me in the face, and you twisted my arm to make me kneel on the floor and pray with you for forgiveness.

SHANNON: I do that, I do that always when I, when . . . I don't have a dime left in my nervous emotional bank account—I can't write a check on it, now.

CHARLOTTE: Larry, let me help you!

MISS FELLOWES [*approaching*]: Charlotte, Charlotte, Charlie!

CHARLOTTE: Help me and let me help you!

SHANNON: The helpless can't help the helpless!

CHARLOTTE: Let me in, Judy's coming!

SHANNON: Let me go. Go away!

[*He thrusts her violently back and rushes into his cubicle, slamming and bolting the door—though the gauze netting is left sticking out. As Miss Fellowes charges onto the verandah, Charlotte runs into the next cubicle, and Hannah moves over from where she has been watching and meets her in the center.*]

MISS FELLOWES: Shannon, Shannon! Where are you?

HANNAH: I think Mr. Shannon has gone down to the beach.

MISS FELLOWES: Was Charlotte Goodall with him? A young blonde girl in our party—was she with him?

HANNAH: No, nobody was with him, he was completely alone.

MISS FELLOWES: I heard a door slam.

HANNAH: That was mine.

MISS FELLOWES [*pointing to the door with the gauze sticking out*]: Is this yours?

HANNAH: Yes, mine. I rushed out to catch the sunset.

[*At this moment Miss Fellowes hears Charlotte sobbing in Hannah's cubicle. She throws the door open.*]

MISS FELLOWES: Charlotte! Come out of there, Charlie! [*She has seized Charlotte by the wrist.*] What's your word worth— nothing? You promised you'd stay away from him! [*Charlotte frees her arm, sobbing bitterly. Miss Fellowes seizes her again, tighter, and starts dragging her away.*] I have talked to your father about this man by long distance and he's getting out a warrant for his arrest, if he dare try coming back to the States after this!

CHARLOTTE: I don't care.

MISS FELLOWES: I do! I'm responsible for you.

CHARLOTTE: I don't want to go back to Texas!

MISS FELLOWES: Yes, you do! And you will!

[*She takes Charlotte firmly by the arm and drags her away behind the hotel. Hannah comes out of her cubicle, where she had gone when Miss Fellowes pulled Charlotte out of it.*]

SHANNON [*from his cubicle*]: Ah, God. . . .

[*Hannah crosses to his cubicle and knocks by the door.*]

HANNAH: The coast is clear now, Mr. Shannon.

[*Shannon does not answer or appear. She sets down her portfolio to pick up Nonno's white linen suit, which she had pressed and hung on the verandah. She crosses to his cubicle with it, and calls in.*]

HANNAH: Nonno? It's almost time for supper! There's going to be a lovely, stormy sunset in a few minutes.

NONNO [*from within*]: Coming!

HANNAH: So is Christmas, Nonno.

NONNO: So is the Fourth of July!

HANNAH: We're past the Fourth of July. Hallowe'en comes next and then Thanksgiving. I hope you'll come forth sooner. [*She lifts the gauze net over his cubicle door.*] Here's your suit, I've pressed it. [*She enters the cubicle.*]

NONNO: It's mighty dark in here, Hannah.

HANNAH: I'll turn the light on for you.

[*Shannon comes out of his cubicle, like the survivor of a plane crash, bringing out with him several pieces of his clerical garb. The black heavy silk bib is loosely fastened about his panting, sweating chest. He hangs over it a heavy gold cross with an amethyst center and attempts to fasten on a starched round collar. Now Hannah comes back out of Nonno's cubicle, adjusting the flowing silk tie which goes with her "artist" costume. For a moment they both face front, adjusting their two outfits. They are like two actors in a play which is about to fold on the road, preparing gravely for a performance which may be the last one.*]

HANNAH [*glancing at Shannon*]: Are you planning to conduct church services of some kind here tonight, Mr. Shannon?

SHANNON: Goddamit, please help me with this! [*He means the round collar.*]

HANNAH [*crossing behind him*]: If you're not going to conduct a church service, why get into that uncomfortable outfit?

SHANNON: Because I've been accused of being defrocked and of lying about it, that's why. I want to show the ladies that I'm still a clocked—*frocked!*—minister of the. . . .

HANNAH: Isn't that lovely gold cross enough to convince the ladies?

SHANNON: No, they know I redeemed it from a Mexico City pawnshop, and they suspect that that's where I got it in the first place.

HANNAH: Hold still just a minute. [*She is behind him, trying to fasten the collar.*] There now, let's hope it stays on. The buttonhole is so frayed I'm afraid that it won't hold the button. [*Her fear is instantly confirmed: the button pops out.*]

SHANNON: Where'd it go?

HANNAH: Here, right under. . . .

[*She picks it up. Shannon rips the collar off, crumples it and hurls it off the verandah. Then he falls into the hammock, panting and twisting. Hannah quietly opens her sketch pad and begins to sketch him. He doesn't at first notice what she is doing.*]

HANNAH [*as she sketches*]: How long have you been inactive in the, uh, Church, Mr. Shannon?

SHANNON: What's that got to do with the price of rice in China?

HANNAH [*gently*]: Nothing.

SHANNON: What's it got to do with the price of coffee beans in Brazil?

HANNAH: I retract the question. With apologies.

SHANNON: To answer your question politely, I have been inactive in the Church for all but one year since I was ordained a minister of the Church.

HANNAH [*sketching rapidly and moving forward a bit to see his face better*]: Well, that's quite a sabbatical, Mr. Shannon.

SHANNON: Yeah, that's . . . quite a . . . sabbatical.

[*Nonno's voice is heard from his cubicle repeating a line of poetry several times.*]

SHANNON: Is your grandfather talking to himself in there?

HANNAH: No, he composes out loud. He has to commit his lines to memory because he can't see to write them or read them.

SHANNON: Sounds like he's stuck on one line.

HANNAH: Yes. I'm afraid his memory is failing. Memory failure is his greatest dread. [*She says this almost coolly, as if it didn't matter.*]

SHANNON: Are you drawing me?

HANNAH: Trying to. You're a very difficult subject. When the Mexican painter Siqueiros did his portrait of the American poet Hart Crane he had to paint him with closed eyes because he couldn't paint his eyes open—there was too much suffering in them and he couldn't paint it.

SHANNON: Sorry, but I'm not going to close my eyes for you. I'm hypnotizing myself—at least trying to—by looking at the light on the orange tree . . . leaves.

HANNAH: That's all right. I can paint your eyes open.

SHANNON: I had one parish one year and then I wasn't defrocked but I was . . . locked out of my church.

HANNAH: Oh . . . Why did they lock you out of it?

SHANNON: Fornication and heresy . . . in the same week.

HANNAH [*sketching rapidly*]: What were the circumstances of the . . . uh . . . first offense?

SHANNON: Yeah, the fornication came first, preceded the heresy by several days. A very young Sunday-school teacher asked to see me privately in my study. A pretty little thing—no chance in the world—only child, and both of her parents were spinsters, almost identical spinsters wearing clothes of the opposite sexes. Fooling some of the people some of the time but not me—none of the time. . . . [*He is pacing the verandah with gathering agitation, and the all-inclusive mockery that his guilt produces.*] Well, she declared herself to me—wildly.

HANNAH: A declaration of love?

SHANNON: Don't make *fun* of me, honey!

HANNAH: I wasn't.

SHANNON: The natural, or unnatural, attraction of one . . . lunatic for . . . another . . . that's all it was. I was the god-damnedest prig in those days that even you could imagine. I said, let's kneel down together and pray and we did, we knelt down, but all of a sudden the kneeling position turned to a reclining position on the rug of my study and . . . When we got up? I struck her. Yes, I did, I struck her in the face and called her a damned little tramp. So she ran home. I heard the next day she'd cut herself with her father's straightblade razor. Yeah, the paternal spinster shaved.

HANNAH: Fatally?

SHANNON: Just broke the skin surface enough to bleed a little, but it made a scandal.

HANNAH: Yes, I can imagine that it . . . provoked some comment.

SHANNON: That it did, it did that. [*He pauses a moment in his fierce pacing as if the recollection still appalled him.*] So the next Sunday when I climbed into the pulpit and looked down over all of those smug, disapproving, accusing faces uplifted, I had an impulse to shake them—so I shook them. I had a prepared sermon—meek, apologetic—I threw it away, tossed it into the chancel. Look here, I said, I shouted, I'm tired of conducting services in praise and worship of a senile delinquent—yeah, that's what I said, I shouted! All your Western theologies, the whole mythology of them, are based on the concept of God as a *senile delinquent* and, by God, I will not and cannot continue to conduct services in praise and worship of this, this . . . this. . . . .

HANNAH [*quietly*]: Senile delinquent?

SHANNON: Yeah, this angry, petulant old man. I mean he's represented like a bad-tempered childish old, old, sick, peevish man—I mean like the sort of old man in a nursing home that's putting together a jigsaw puzzle and can't put it together and gets furious at it and kicks over the table. Yes, I tell you they *do* that, all our theologies do it—accuse God of being a cruel, senile delinquent, blaming the world and brutally punishing all he created for his own faults in construction, and then, ha-ha, yeah—a thunderstorm broke that Sunday. . . .

HANNAH: You mean *outside* the church?

SHANNON: Yep, it was wilder than I was! And out they slithered, they slithered out of their pews to their shiny black cockroach sedans, ha-ha, and I shouted after them, hell, I even followed them halfway out of the church, shouting after them as they. . . . [*He stops with a gasp for breath.*]

HANNAH: Slithered out?

SHANNON: I shouted after them, go on, go home and close your house windows, all your windows and doors, against the truth about God!

HANNAH: Oh, my heavens. Which is just what they did—poor things.

SHANNON: Miss Jelkes honey, Pleasant Valley, Virginia, was an exclusive suburb of a large city and these poor things were not poor—materially speaking.

HANNAH [*smiling a bit*]: What was the, uh, upshot of it?

SHANNON: Upshot of it? Well, I wasn't defrocked. I was just locked out of the church in Pleasant Valley, Virginia, and put in a nice little private asylum to recuperate from a complete nervous breakdown as they preferred to regard it, and then, and then I . . . I entered my present line—tours of God's world conducted by a minister of God with a cross and a round collar to prove it. Collecting evidence!

HANNAH: Evidence of what, Mr. Shannon?

SHANNON [*a touch shyly now*]: My personal idea of God, not as a senile delinquent, but as a. . . .

HANNAH: Incomplete sentence.

SHANNON: It's going to storm tonight—a terrific electric storm. Then you will see the Reverend T. Lawrence Shannon's conception of God Almighty paying a visit to the world he created. I want to go back to the Church and preach the gospel of God as Lightning and Thunder . . . and also stray dogs vivisected and . . . and . . . and. . . . [*He points out suddenly toward the sea.*] That's him! There he is now! [*He is pointing out at a blaze, a majestic apocalypse of gold light, shafting the sky as the sun drops into the Pacific.*] His oblivious majesty—and *here I am* on this . . . dilapidated verandah of a cheap hotel, out of season, in a country caught and destroyed in its flesh and corrupted in its spirit by its gold-hungry conquistadors that bore the flag of the Inquisition along with the Cross of Christ. Yes . . . and. . . . [*There is a pause.*]

HANNAH: Mr. Shannon . . . ?

SHANNON: Yes . . . ?

HANNAH [*smiling a little*]: I have a strong feeling you will go back to the Church with this evidence you've been collecting, but when you do and it's a black Sunday morning, look out over the congregation, over the smug, complacent faces for a few old, very old faces, looking up at you, as you begin your sermon, with eyes like a piercing cry for something to still look up to, something to still believe in. And then I think you'll not shout what you say you shouted that black Sunday in Pleasant Valley, Virginia. I think you will throw away the violent, furious sermon, you'll toss *it* into the chancel, and talk about . . . no, maybe talk about . . . nothing . . . just. . . .

SHANNON: What?

HANNAH: Lead them beside still waters because you know how badly they need the still waters, Mr. Shannon.

[*There is a moment of silence between them.*]

SHANNON: Lemme see that thing. [*He seizes the sketch pad from her and is visibly impressed by what he sees. There is another moment which is prolonged to Hannah's embarrassment.*]

HANNAH: Where did you say the patrona put your party of ladies?

SHANNON: She had her . . . Mexican concubines put their luggage in the annex.

HANNAH: Where is the annex?

SHANNON: Right down the hill back of here, but all of my ladies except the teen-age Medea and the older Medea have gone out in a glass-bottomed boat to observe the . . . submarine marvels.

HANNAH: Well, when they come back to the annex they're going to observe my water colors with some marvelous submarine prices marked on the mattings.

SHANNON: By God, you're a hustler, aren't you, you're a fantastic cool hustler.

HANNAH: Yes, like *you*, Mr. Shannon. [*She gently removes her sketch pad from his grasp.*] Oh, Mr. Shannon, if Nonno, Grandfather, comes out of his cell number 4 before I get back, will you please look out for him for me? I won't be longer than three shakes of a lively sheep's tail. [*She snatches up her portfolio and goes briskly off the verandah.*]

SHANNON: Fantastic, absolutely fantastic.

[*There is a windy sound in the rain forest and a flicker of gold light like a silent scattering of gold coins on the verandah; then the sound of shouting voices. The Mexican boys appear with a wildly agitated creature—a captive iguana tied up in a shirt. They crouch down by the cactus clumps that are growing below the verandah and hitch the iguana to a post with a piece of rope. Maxine is attracted by the commotion and appears on the verandah above them.*]

PEDRO: Tenemos fiesta!*

PANCHO: Comeremos bien.

PEDRO: Damela, damela! Yo la ataré.

PANCHO: *Yo* la cojí—*yo* la ataré!

PEDRO: Lo que vas a *hacer* es dejarla escapar.

MAXINE: Ammarla fuerte! Ole, ole! No la dejes escapar. Dejala moverse! [*To Shannon.*] They caught an iguana.

SHANNON: I've noticed they did that, Maxine.

---

*We're going to have a feast! / We'll eat good! / Give it to me! I'll tie it up. / I caught it—*I'll* tie it up! / You'll only let it get away. / Tie it up tight! Ole, ole! Don't let it get away. Give it enough room!

[*She is holding her drink deliberately close to him. The Germans have heard the commotion and crowd onto the verandah. Frau Fahrenkopf rushes over to Maxine.*]

FRAU FAHRENKOPF: What is this? What's going on? A snake? Did they catch a snake?

MAXINE: No. *Lizard.*

FRAU FAHRENKOPF [*with exaggerated revulsion*]: Ouuu . . . lizard! [*She strikes a grotesque attitude of terror as if she were threatened by Jack the Ripper.*]

SHANNON [*to Maxine*]: You like iguana meat, don't you?

FRAU FAHRENKOPF: Eat? *Eat?* A big *lizard?*

MAXINE: Yep, they're mighty good eating—taste like white meat of chicken.

[*Frau Fahrenkopf rushes back to her family. They talk excitedly in German about the iguana.*]

SHANNON: If you mean Mexican chicken, that's no recommendation. Mexican chickens are scavengers and they taste like what they scavenge.

MAXINE: Naw, I mean Texas chicken.

SHANNON [*dreamily*]: Texas . . . chicken. . . .

[*He paces restlessly down the verandah. Maxine divides her attention between his tall, lean figure, that seems incapable of stillness, and the wriggling bodies of the Mexican boys lying on their stomachs half under the verandah—as if she were mentally comparing two opposite attractions to her simple, sensual nature. Shannon turns at the end of the verandah and sees her eyes fixed on him.*]

SHANNON: What is the sex of this iguana, Maxine?

MAXINE: Hah, who cares about the sex of an iguana . . . [*He passes close by her.*] . . . except another . . . iguana?

SHANNON: Haven't you heard the limerick about iguanas? [*He removes her drink from her hand and it seems as if he might drink it, but he only sniffs it, with an expression of repugnance. She chuckles.*]

> There was a young gaucho named Bruno
> Who said about love, This I do know:
> Women are fine, and sheep are divine,
> But iguanas are—*Numero Uno!*

[*On "Numero Uno" Shannon empties Maxine's drink over the railing, deliberately onto the humped, wriggling posterior of Pedro, who springs up with angry protests.*]

PEDRO: Me cágo . . . hijo de la . . .

SHANNON: Qué? Qué?

MAXINE: Véte!

[*Shannon laughs viciously. The iguana escapes and both boys rush shouting after it. One of them dives on it and recaptures it at the edge of the jungle.*]

PANCHO: La iguana se escapé.*

MAXINE: Cojela, cojela! La cojíste? Si no la cojes, te morderá el culo. La cojíste?

PEDRO: La cojí.

[*The boys wiggle back under the verandah with the iguana.*]

---

* The iguana's escaped. / Get it, get it! Have you got it? If you don't, it'll bite your behind. Have you got it? / He's got it.

MAXINE [*returning to Shannon*]: I thought you were gonna break down and take a drink, Reverend.

SHANNON: Just the odor of liquor makes me feel nauseated.

MAXINE: You couldn't smell it if you got it *in* you. [*She touches his sweating forehead. He brushes her hand off like an insect.*] Hah! [*She crosses over to the liquor cart, and he looks after her with a sadistic grin.*]

SHANNON: Maxine honey, whoever told you that you look good in tight pants was not a sincere friend of yours.

[*He turns away. At the same instant, a crash and a hoarse, started outcry are heard from Nonno's cubicle.*]

MAXINE: I knew it, I *knew* it! The old man's took a fall!

[*Shannon rushes into the cubicle, followed by Maxine.*

[*The light has been gradually, steadily dimming during the incident of the iguana's escape. There is, in effect, a division of scenes here, though it is accomplished without a blackout or curtain. As Shannon and Maxine enter Nonno's cubicle, Herr Fahrenkopf appears on the now twilit verandah. He turns on an outsize light fixture that is suspended from overhead, a full pearly-moon of a light globe that gives an unearthly luster to the scene. The great pearly globe is decorated by night insects, large but gossamer moths that have immolated themselves on its surface: the light through their wings gives them an opalescent color, a touch of fantasy.*]

[*Now Shannon leads the old poet out of his cubicle, onto the facing verandah. The old man is impeccably dressed in snow-white linen with a black string tie. His leonine mane of hair gleams like silver as he passes under the globe.*]

NONNO: No bones broke, I'm made out of India rubber!

SHANNON: A traveler-born falls down many times in his travels.

NONNO: Hannah? [*His vision and other senses have so far deteriorated that he thinks he is being led out by Hannah.*] I'm pretty sure I'm going to finish it here.

SHANNON [*shouting, gently*]: I've got the same feeling, Grampa.

[*Maxine follows them out of the cubicle.*]

NONNO: I've never been surer of anything in my life.

SHANNON [*gently and wryly*]: I've never been surer of anything in mine either.

[*Herr Fahrenkopf has been listening with an expression of entrancement to his portable radio, held close to his ear, the sound unrealistically low. Now he turns it off and makes an excited speech.*]

HERR FAHRENKOPF: The London fires have spread all the way from the heart of London to the Channel coast! Goering, Field Marshall Goering, calls it "the new phase of conquest!" *Superfirebombs! Each night!*

[*Nonno catches only the excited tone of this announcement and interprets it as a request for a recitation. He strikes the floor with his cane, throws back his silver-maned head and begins the delivery in a grand, declamatory style.*]

NONNO:

> Youth must be wanton, youth must be quick,
> Dance to the candle while lasteth the wick,
>
> Youth must be foolish and. . . .

[*Nonno falters on the line, a look of confusion and fear on his face. The Germans are amused. Wolfgang goes up to Nonno and shouts into his face.*]

WOLFGANG: Sir? What is your age? How old?

[*Hannah, who has just returned to the verandah, rushes up to her grandfather and answers for him.*]

HANNAH: He is ninety-seven years *young!*

HERR FAHRENKOPF: How old?

HANNAH: Ninety-seven—almost a *century young!*

[*Herr Fahrenkopf repeats this information to his beaming wife and Hilda in German.*]

NONNO [*cutting in on the Germans*]:
> Youth must be foolish and mirthful and blind,
> Gaze not before and glance not behind,

> Mark not. . . .

[*He falters again.*]

HANNAH [*prompting him, holding tightly onto his arm*]:
> Mark not the shadow that darkens the way—

[*They recite the next lines together.*]
> Regret not the glitter of any lost day,

> But laugh with no reason except the red wine,
> For youth must be youthful and foolish and blind!

[*The Germans are loudly amused. Wolfgang applauds directly in the old poet's face. Nonno makes a little unsteady bow, leaning forward precariously on his cane. Shannon takes a firm hold of his arm as Hannah turns to the Germans, opening her portfolio of sketches and addressing Wolfgang.*]

HANNAH: Am I right in thinking you are on your honeymoon? [*There is no response, and she repeats the question in German while Frau Fahrenkopf laughs and nods vehemently.*] Habe ich recht dass Sie auf Ihrer Hochzeitsreise sind? Was für eine hübsche junge Braut! Ich mache Pastell-Skizzen . . . darf ich, würden Sie mir erlauben . . . ? Wurden Sie, bitte . . . bitte. . . .

[*Herr Fahrenkopf bursts into a Nazi marching song and leads his party to the champagne bucket on the table at the left. Shannon has steered Nonno to the other table.*]

NONNO [*exhilarated*]: Hannah! What was the *take*?

HANNAH [*embarrassed*]: Grandfather, sit down, please stop shouting!

NONNO: Hah? Did they cross your palm with silver or paper, Hannah?

HANNAH [*almost desperately*]: Nonno! No more shouting! Sit down at the table. It's time to *eat!*

SHANNON: Chow time, Grampa.

NONNO [*confused but still shouting*]: How much did they come across with?

HANNAH: Nonno! *Please!*

NONNO: Did they, did you . . . sell 'em a . . . water color?

HANNAH: No sale, Grandfather!

MAXINE: Hah!

[*Hannah turns to Shannon, her usual composure shattered, or nearly so.*]

HANNAH: He won't sit down or stop shouting.

NONNO [*blinking and beaming with the grotesque suggestion of an old coquette*]: Hah? How rich did we strike it, Hannah?

SHANNON: *You* sit down, Miss Jelkes. [*He says it with gentle authority, to which she yields. He takes hold of the old man's forearm and places in his hand a crumpled Mexican bill.*] Sir? Sir? [*He is shouting.*] Five! Dollars! I'm putting it in your pocket.

HANNAH: We can't accept . . . gratuities, Mr. Shannon.

SHANNON: Hell, I gave him five pesos.

NONNO: Mighty good for one poem!

SHANNON: Sir? Sir? The *pecuniary rewards* of a *poem* are *grossly inferior* to its *merits, always!*

[*He is being fiercely, almost mockingly tender with the old man—a thing we are when the pathos of the old, the ancient, the dying is such a wound to our own (savagely beleaguered) nerves and sensibilities that this outside demand on us is beyond our collateral, our emotional reserve. This is as true of Hannah as it is of Shannon, of course. They have both overdrawn their reserves at this point of the encounter between them.*]

NONNO: Hah? Yes. . . . [*He is worn out now, but still shouting.*] We're going to clean up in this place!

SHANNON: You bet you're going to clean up here!

[*Maxine utters her one-note bark of a laugh. Shannon throws a hard roll at her. She wanders amiably back toward the German table.*]

NONNO [*tottering, panting, hanging onto Shannon's arm, thinking it is Hannah's*]: Is the, the . . . dining room . . . *crowded?* [*He looks blindly about with wild surmise.*]

SHANNON: Yep, it's filled to capacity! There's a big crowd at the door! [*His voice doesn't penetrate the old man's deafness.*]

NONNO: If there's a cocktail lounge, Hannah, we ought to . . . work that . . . first. Strike while the iron is hot, ho, ho, while it's hot. . . . [*This is like a delirium—only as strong a woman as Hannah could remain outwardly impassive.*]

HANNAH: He thinks you're me, Mr. Shannon. Help him into a chair. Please stay with him a minute, I. . . .

[*She moves away from the table and breathes as if she has just been dragged up half-drowned from the sea. Shannon eases the old man into a chair. Almost at once Nonno's feverish vitality collapses and he starts drifting back toward half sleep.*]

SHANNON [*crossing to* HANNAH]: What're you breathing like that for?

HANNAH: Some people take a drink, some take a pill. I just take a few deep breaths.

SHANNON: You're making too much out of this. It's a natural thing in a man as old as Grampa.

HANNAH: I know, I know. He's had more than one of these little "cerebral accidents" as you call them, and all in the last few months. He was amazing till lately. I had to show his passport to prove that he was the oldest living and practicing poet on earth. We did well, we made expenses and *more!* But . . . when I saw he was failing, I tried to persuade him to go back to Nantucket, but he conducts our tours. He said, "No, *Mexico!*" So here we are on this windy hilltop like a pair of scarecrows. . . . The bus from Mexico City broke down at an altitude of 15,000 feet above sea level. That's when I think the latest cerebral incident happened. It isn't so much the loss of hearing and sight but the . . . dimming out of the mind that I can't bear, because until lately, just lately, his mind was amazingly clear. But yesterday? In Taxco? I spent nearly all we had left on the wheelchair for him and still he insisted that we go on with the trip till we got to the sea, the . . . cradle of life as he calls it. . . . [*She suddenly notices Nonno, sunk in his chair as if lifeless. She draws a sharp breath, and goes quietly to him.*]

SHANNON [*to the Mexican boys*]: Servicio! Aqui! [*The force of his order proves effective: they serve the fish course.*]

HANNAH: What a kind man you are. I don't know how to thank you, Mr. Shannon. I'm going to wake him up now. Nonno! [*She claps her hands quietly at his ear. The old man rouses with a confused, breathless chuckle.*] Nonno, linen napkins. [*She removes a napkin from the pocket of her smock.*] I always carry one with me, you see, in case we run into paper napkins as sometimes happens, you see. . . .

NONNO: Wonderful place here. . . . I hope it is à la carte, Hannah, I want a very light supper so I won't get sleepy. I'm going to work after supper. I'm going to finish it here.

HANNAH: Nonno? We've made a friend here. Nonno, this is the Reverend Mr. Shannon.

NONNO [*struggling out of his confusion*]: Reverend?

HANNAH [*shouting to him*]: Mr. Shannon's an Episcopal clergyman, Nonno.

NONNO: A man of God?

HANNAH: A man of God, on vacation.

NONNO: Hannah, tell him I'm too old to baptize and too young to bury but on the market for marriage to a rich widow, fat, fair and forty.

[*Nonno is delighted by all of his own little jokes. One can see him exchanging these pleasantries with the rocking-chair brigades of summer hotels at the turn of the century—and with professors' wives at little colleges in New England. But now it has become somewhat grotesque in a touching way, this desire to please, this playful manner, these venerable jokes. Shannon goes along with it. The old man touches something in him which is outside of his concern with himself. This part of the scene, which is played in a "scherzo" mood, has an accompanying windy obligato on the hilltop—all through it we hear the wind from the sea gradually rising, sweeping up the hill through the rain forest, and there are fitful glimmers of lightning in the sky.*]

NONNO: But very few ladies ever go past forty if you believe 'em, ho, ho! Ask him to . . . give the blessing. Mexican food needs blessing.

SHANNON: Sir, you give the blessing. I'll be right with you. [*He has broken one of his shoelaces.*]

NONNO: Tell him I will oblige him on one condition.

SHANNON: What condition, sir?

NONNO: That you'll keep my daughter company when I retire after dinner. I go to bed with the chickens and get up with the roosters, ho, ho! So you're a man of God. A benedict or a bachelor?

SHANNON: Bachelor, sir. No sane and civilized woman would have me, Mr. Coffin.

NONNO: What did he say, Hannah?

HANNAH [*embarrassed*]: Nonno, give the blessing.

NONNO [*not hearing this*]: I call her my daughter, but she's my

71

daughter's daughter. We've been in charge of each other since she lost both her parents in the very first automobile crash on the island of Nantucket.

HANNAH: Nonno, give the blessing.

NONNO: She isn't a modern flapper, she isn't modern and she—doesn't flap, but she was brought up to be a wonderful wife and mother. But . . . I'm a selfish old man so I've kept her all to myself.

HANNAH [*shouting into his ear*]: Nonno, Nonno, the blessing!

NONNO [*rising with an effort*]: Yes, the blessing. Bless this food to our use, and ourselves to Thy service. Amen. [*He totters back into his chair.*]

SHANNON: Amen.

[*Nonno's mind starts drifting, his head drooping forward. He murmurs to himself.*]

SHANNON: How good is the old man's poetry?

HANNAH: My grandfather was a fairly well-known minor poet before the First World War and for a little while after.

SHANNON: In the minor league, huh?

HANNAH: Yes, a minor league poet with a major league spirit. I'm proud to be his granddaughter. . . . [*She draws a pack of cigarettes from her pocket, then replaces it immediately without taking a cigarette.*]

NONNO [*very confused*]: Hannah, it's too hot for . . . hot cereals this . . . morning. . . . [*He shakes his head several times with a rueful chuckle.*]

HANNAH: He's not quite back, you see, he thinks it's morning. [*She says this as if making an embarrassing admission, with a quick, frightened smile at Shannon.*]

SHANNON: Fantastic—*fantastic*.

HANNAH: That word "fantastic" seems to be your favorite word, Mr. Shannon.

SHANNON [*looking out gloomily from the verandah*]: Yeah, well, you know we—live on two levels, Miss Jelkes, the realistic level and the fantastic level, and which is the real one, really. . . .

HANNAH: I would say both, Mr. Shannon.

SHANNON: But when you live on the fantastic level as I have lately but have got to operate on the realistic level, that's when you're spooked, that's the spook. . . . [*This is said as if it were a private reflection.*] I thought I'd shake the spook here but conditions have changed here. I didn't know the patrona had turned to a widow, a sort of bright widow spider. [*He chuckles almost like Nonno.*]

[*Maxine has pushed one of those gay little brass-and-glass liquor carts around the corner of the verandah. It is laden with an ice bucket, coconuts and a variety of liquors. She hums gaily to herself as she pushes the cart close to the table.*]

MAXINE: Cocktails, anybody?

HANNAH: No, thank you, Mrs. Faulk, I don't think we care for any.

SHANNON: People don't drink cocktails between the fish and the entrée, Maxine honey.

MAXINE: Grampa needs a toddy to wake him up. Old folks need a toddy to pick 'em up. [*She shouts into the old man's ear.*] Grampa! How about a toddy? [*Her hips are thrust out at Shannon.*]

SHANNON: Maxine, your ass—excuse me, Miss Jelkes—your hips, Maxine, are too fat for this verandah.

MAXINE: Hah! Mexicans like 'em, if I can judge by the pokes and pinches I get in the buses to town. And so do the Germans. Ev'ry time I go near Herr Fahrenkopf he gives me a pinch or a goose.

SHANNON: Then go near him again for another goose.

MAXINE: Hah! I'm mixing Grampa a Manhattan with two cherries in it so he'll live through dinner.

SHANNON: Go on back to your Nazis, I'll mix the Manhattan for him. [*He goes to the liquor cart.*]

MAXINE [*to Hannah*]: How about you, honey, a little soda with lime juice?

HANNAH: Nothing for me, thank you.

SHANNON: Don't make nervous people more nervous, Maxine.

MAXINE: You better let me mix that toddy for Grampa, you're making a mess of it, Shannon.

[*With a snort of fury, he thrusts the liquor cart like a battering ram at her belly. Some of the bottles fall off it; she thrusts it right back at him.*]

HANNAH: Mrs. Faulk, Mr. Shannon, this is childish, please stop it!

[*The Germans are attracted by the disturbance. They cluster around, laughing delightedly. Shannon and Maxine seize opposite ends of the rolling liquor cart and thrust it toward each other, both grinning fiercely as gladiators in mortal combat. The Germans shriek with laughter and chatter in German.*]

HANNAH: Mr. Shannon, stop it! [*She appeals to the Germans.*] *Bitte!* Nehmen Sie die Spirituosen weg. Bitte, nehmen Sie sie weg.

[*Shannon has wrested the cart from Maxine and pushed it at the Germans. They scream delightedly. The cart crashes into the wall of the verandah. Shannon leaps down the steps and runs into the foliage. Birds scream in the rain forest. Then sudden quiet returns to the verandah as the Germans go back to their own table.*]

MAXINE: Crazy, black Irish Protestant son of a . . . Protestant!

HANNAH: Mrs. Faulk, he's putting up a struggle not to drink.

MAXINE: Don't interfere. You're an interfering woman.

HANNAH: Mr. Shannon is dangerously . . . disturbed.

MAXINE: I know how to handle him, honey—you just met him today. Here's Grampa's Manhattan cocktail with two cherries in it.

HANNAH: Please don't call him Grampa.

MAXINE: Shannon calls him Grampa.

HANNAH [*taking the drink*]: He doesn't make it sound condescending, but you *do*. My grandfather is a gentleman in the true sense of the word, he is a *gentle man.*

MAXINE: What are you?

HANNAH: I am his granddaughter.

MAXINE: Is that all you are?

HANNAH: I think it's enough to be.

MAXINE: Yeah, but you're also a deadbeat, using that dying old man for a front to get in places without the cash to pay even one day in advance. Why, you're dragging him around with you like Mexican beggars carry around a sick baby to put the touch on the tourists.

HANNAH: I told you I had no money.

MAXINE: Yes, and I told you that I was a widow—recent. In such a financial hole they might as well have buried me with my husband.

[*Shannon reappears from the jungle foliage but remains unnoticed by Hannah and Maxine.*]

HANNAH [*with forced calm*]: Tomorrow morning, at daybreak, I will go in town. I will set up my easel in the plaza and peddle my water colors and sketch tourists. I am not a weak person, my failure here isn't typical of me.

MAXINE: I'm not a weak person either.

HANNAH: No. By no means, no. Your strength is awe-inspiring.

MAXINE: You're goddam right about that, but how do you think you'll get to Acapulco without the cabfare or even the busfare there?

HANNAH: I will go on shanks' mare, Mrs. Faulk—islanders are good walkers. And if you doubt my word for it, if you really think I came here as a deadbeat, then I will put my grandfather back in his wheelchair and push him back down this hill to the road and all the way back into town.

MAXINE: Ten miles, with a storm coming up?

HANNAH: Yes, I would—I will. [*She is dominating Maxine in this exchange. Both stand beside the table. Nonno's head is drooping back into sleep.*]

MAXINE: I wouldn't let you.

HANNAH: But you've made it clear that you don't want us to stay here for one night even.

MAXINE: The storm would blow that old man out of his wheel-chair like a dead leaf.

HANNAH: He would prefer that to staying where he's not wel-come, and I would prefer it for him, and for myself, Mrs. Faulk. [*She turns to the Mexican boys.*] Where is his wheelchair? Where is my grandfather's wheelchair?

[*This exchange has roused the old man. He struggles up from his chair, confused, strikes the floor with his cane and starts declaiming a poem.*]

NONNO:

>Love's an old remembered song
>A drunken fiddler plays,
>Stumbling crazily along
>Crooked alleyways.
>
>When his heart is mad with music
>He will play the—

HANNAH: Nonno, not now, Nonno! He thought someone asked for a poem. [*She gets him back into the chair. Hannah and Maxine are still unaware of Shannon.*]

MAXINE: Calm down, honey.

HANNAH: I'm perfectly calm, Mrs. Faulk.

MAXINE: I'm *not*. That's the trouble.

HANNAH: I understand that, Mrs. Faulk. You lost your husband just lately. I think you probably miss him more than you know.

MAXINE: No, the trouble is Shannon.

HANNAH: You mean his nervous state and his . . . ?

MAXINE: No, I just mean Shannon. I want you to lay off him, honey. You're not for Shannon and Shannon isn't for you.

HANNAH: Mrs. Faulk, I'm a New England spinster who is pushing forty.

MAXINE: I got the vibrations between you—I'm very good at catching vibrations between people—and there sure was a vibration between you and Shannon the moment you got here. That, just that, believe me, nothing but that has made this . . . misunderstanding between us. So if you just don't mess with Shannon, you and your Grampa can stay on here as long as you want to, honey.

HANNAH: Oh, Mrs. Faulk, do I look like a *vamp?*

MAXINE: They come in all types. I've had all types of them here.

[*Shannon comes over to the table.*]

SHANNON: Maxine, I told you don't make nervous people more nervous, but you wouldn't listen.

MAXINE: What you need is a drink.

SHANNON: Let me decide about that.

HANNAH: Won't you sit down with us, Mr. Shannon, and eat something? Please. You'll feel better.

SHANNON: I'm not hungry right now.

HANNAH: Well, just sit down with us, won't you?

[*Shannon sits down with Hannah.*]

MAXINE [*warningly to Hannah*]: O.K. O.K. . . .

NONNO [*rousing a bit and mumbling*]: Wonderful . . . wonderful place here.

[*Maxine retires from the table and wheels the liquor cart over to the German party.*]

SHANNON: Would you have gone through with it?

HANNAH: Haven't you ever played poker, Mr. Shannon?

SHANNON: You mean you were bluffing?

HANNAH: Let's say I was drawing to an inside straight. [*The wind rises and sweeps up the hill like a great waking sigh from the ocean.*] It *is* going to storm. I hope your ladies aren't still out in that, that . . . glass-bottomed boat, observing the, uh, submarine . . . marvels.

SHANNON: That's because you don't know these ladies. However, they're back from the boat trip. They're down at the cantina, dancing together to the jukebox and hatching new plots to get me kicked out of Blake Tours.

HANNAH: What would you do if you. . . .

SHANNON: Got the sack? Go back to the Church or take the long swim to China. [*Hannah removes a crumpled pack of cigarettes from her pocket. She discovers only two left in the pack and decides to save them for later. She returns the pack to her pocket.*] May I have one of your cigarettes, Miss Jelkes? [*She offers him the pack. He takes it from her and crumples it and throws it off the verandah.*] Never smoke those, they're made out of tobacco from cigarette stubs that beggars pick up off sidewalks and out of gutters in Mexico City. [*He produces a tin of English cigarettes.*] Have these—Benson and Hedges, imported, in an airtight tin, my luxury in my life.

HANNAH: Why—thank you, I will, since you have thrown mine away.

SHANNON: I'm going to tell you something about yourself. You are a lady, a *real* one and a *great* one.

HANNAH: What have I done to merit that compliment from you?

SHANNON: It isn't a compliment, it's just a report on what I've noticed about you at a time when it's hard for me to notice anything outside myself. You took out those Mexican cigarettes, you found you just had two left, you can't afford to buy a new pack of even that cheap brand, so you put them away for later. Right?

HANNAH: Mercilessly accurate, Mr. Shannon.

SHANNON: But when I asked you for one, you offered it to me without a sign of reluctance.

HANNAH: Aren't you making a big point out of a small matter?

SHANNON: Just the opposite, honey, I'm making a small point out of a very large matter. [*Shannon has put a cigarette in his lips but has no matches. Hannah has some and she lights his cigarette for him.*] How'd you learn how to light a match in the wind?

HANNAH: Oh, I've learned lots of useful little things like that. I wish I'd learned some *big* ones.

SHANNON: Such as what?

HANNAH: How to help you, Mr. Shannon. . . .

SHANNON: Now I know why I came here!

HANNAH: To meet someone who can light a match in the wind?

SHANNON [*looking down at the table, his voice choking*]: To meet someone who wants to *help* me, Miss Jelkes. . . . [*He makes a quick, embarrassed turn in the chair, as if to avoid her seeing that he has tears in his eyes. She regards him steadily and tenderly, as she would her grandfather.*]

HANNAH: Has it been so long since anyone has wanted to help you, or have you just. . . .

SHANNON: Have I—what?

HANNAH: Just been so much involved with a struggle in yourself that you haven't noticed when people have wanted to help you, the little they can? I know people torture each other many times like devils, but sometimes they do see and know each other, you know, and then, if they're decent, they do want to help each other all that they can. Now will you please help *me*? Take care of Nonno while I remove my water colors from the annex verandah because the storm is coming up by leaps and bounds now.

[*He gives a quick, jerky nod, dropping his face briefly into the cup of his hands. She murmurs "Thank you" and springs up, starting along the verandah. Halfway across, as the storm closes in upon the hilltop with a thunderclap and a sound of rain coming, Hannah turns to look back at the table. Shannon has risen and gone around the table to Nonno.*]

SHANNON: Grampa? Nonno? Let's get up before the rain hits us, Grampa.

NONNO: What? What?

[*Shannon gets the old man out of his chair and shepherds him to the back of the verandah as Hannah rushes toward the annex. The Mexican boys hastily clear the table, fold it up and lean it against the wall. Shannon and Nonno turn and face toward the*] *storm, like brave men facing a firing squad. Maxine is excitedly giving orders to the boys.*]

MAXINE: Pronto, pronto, muchachos! Pronto, pronto! Llevaros todas las cosas! Pronto, pronto! Recoje los platos! Apurate con el mantel!*

PEDRO: Nos estamos dando prisa!

PANCHO: Que el chubasco lave los platos!

[*The German party look on the storm as a Wagnerian climax. They rise from their table as the boys come to clear it, and start singing exultantly. The storm, with its white convulsions of light, is like a giant white bird attacking the hilltop of the Costa Verde. Hannah reappears with her water colors clutched against her chest.*]

SHANNON: Got them?

HANNAH: Yes, just in time. Here is your God, Mr. Shannon.

SHANNON [*quietly*]: Yes, I see him, I hear him, I know him. And if he doesn't know that I know him, let him strike me dead with a bolt of his lightning.

[*He moves away from the wall to the edge of the verandah as a fine silver sheet of rain descends off the sloping roof, catching the light and dimming the figures behind it. Now everything is silver, delicately lustrous. Shannon extends his hands under the rainfall, turning them in it as if to cool them. Then he cups them to catch the water in his palms and bathes his forehead with it. The rainfall increases. The sound of the marimba band at the beach cantina is brought up the hill by the wind. Shan-*

_____

*Hurry, hurry, boys! Pick everything up! Get the plates! Hurry with the table cloth! / We *are* hurrying! / Let the storm wash the plates!

non lowers his hands from his burning forehead and stretches them out through the rain's silver sheet as if he were reaching for something outside and beyond himself. Then nothing is visible but these reaching-out hands. A pure white flash of lightning reveals Hannah and Nonno against the wall, behind Shannon, and the electric globe suspended from the roof goes out, the power extinguished by the storm. A clear shaft of light stays on Shannon's reaching-out hands till the stage curtain has fallen, slowly.]*

INTERMISSION

*Note: In staging, the plastic elements should be restrained so that they don't take precedence over the more important human values. It should not seem like an "effect curtain." The faint, windy music of the marimba band from the cantina should continue as the houselights are brought up for the intermission.

ACT THREE

The verandah, several hours later. Cubicles number 3, 4, and 5 are dimly lighted within. We see Hannah in number 3, and Nonno in number 4. Shannon, who has taken off his shirt, is seated at a table on the verandah, writing a letter to his bishop. All but this table have been folded and stacked against the wall and Maxine is putting the hammock back up which had been taken down for dinner. The electric power is still off and the cubicles are lighted by oil lamps. The sky has cleared completely, the moon is making for full and it bathes the scene in an almost garish silver which is intensified by the wetness from the recent rainstorm. Everything is drenched—there are pools of silver here and there on the floor of the verandah. At one side a smudge-pot is burning to repel the mosquitoes, which are particularly vicious after a tropical downpour when the wind is exhausted.

Shannon is working feverishly on the letter to the bishop, now and then slapping at a mosquito on his bare torso. He is shiny with perspiration, still breathing like a spent runner, muttering to himself as he writes and sometimes suddenly drawing a loud deep breath and simultaneously throwing back his head to stare up wildly at the night sky. Hannah is seated on a straight-back chair behind the mosquito netting in her cubicle—very straight herself, holding a small book in her hands but looking steadily over it at Shannon, like a guardian angel. Her hair has been let down. Nonno can be seen in his cubicle rocking back and forth on the edge of the narrow bed as he goes over and over the lines of his first new poem in "twenty-some years"—which he knows is his last one.

Now and then the sound of distant music drifts up from the beach cantina.

MAXINE: Workin' on your sermon for next Sunday, Rev'rend?

SHANNON: I'm writing a very important letter, Maxine. [*He means don't disturb me.*]

MAXINE: Who to, Shannon?

SHANNON: The Dean of the Divinity School at Sewanee. [*Maxine repeats "Sewanee" to herself, tolerantly.*] Yes, and I'd appreciate it very much, Maxine honey, if you'd get Pedro or Pancho to drive into town with it tonight so it will go out first thing in the morning.

MAXINE: The kids took off in the station wagon already—for some cold beers and hot whores at the cantina.

SHANNON: "Fred's dead"—he's lucky. . . .

MAXINE: Don't misunderstand me about Fred, baby. I miss him, but we'd not only stopped sleeping together, we'd stopped talking together except in grunts—no quarrels, no misunderstandings, but if we exchanged two grunts in the course of a day, it was a long conversation we'd had that day between us.

SHANNON: Fred knew when I was spooked—wouldn't have to tell him. He'd just look at me and say, "Well, Shannon, you're spooked."

MAXINE: Yeah, well, Fred and me'd reached the point of just grunting.

SHANNON: Maybe he thought you'd turned into a pig, Maxine.

MAXINE: Hah! You know damn well that Fred respected me, Shannon, like I did Fred. We just, well, you know . . . age difference. . . .

SHANNON: Well, you've got Pedro and Pancho.

MAXINE: Employees. They don't respect me enough. When you let employees get too free with you, personally, they stop respecting you, Shannon. And it's, well, it's . . . humiliating—not to be . . . respected.

SHANNON: Then take more bus trips to town for the Mexican pokes and the pinches, or get Herr Fahrenkopf to "respect" you, honey.

MAXINE: Hah! You kill me. I been thinking lately of selling out here and going back to the States, to Texas, and operating a tourist camp outside some live town like Houston or Dallas, on a highway, and renting out cabins to business executives wanting a comfortable little intimate little place to give a little after-hours dictation to their cute little secretaries that can't type or write shorthand. Complimentary rum-cocos—bathrooms with bidets. I'll introduce the bidet to the States.

SHANNON: Does everything have to wind up on that level with you, Maxine?

MAXINE: Yes and no, baby. I know the difference between loving someone and just sleeping with someone—even I know about that. [*He starts to rise.*] We've both reached a point where we've got to settle for something that works for us in our lives—even if it isn't on the highest kind of level.

SHANNON: I don't want to rot.

MAXINE: You wouldn't. I wouldn't let you! I know your psychological history. I remember one of your conversations on this verandah with Fred. You was explaining to him how your problems first started. You told him that Mama, your Mama, used to send you to bed before you was ready to sleep—so you practiced the little boy's vice, you amused yourself with yourself. And once she caught you at it and whaled your backside with the back side of a hairbrush because she said she had to punish you for it because it made God mad as much as it did Mama, and she had to punish you for it so God wouldn't punish you for it harder than she would.

SHANNON: I was talking to Fred.

MAXINE: Yeah, but I heard it, all of it. You said you loved God and Mama and so you quit it to please them, but it was your secret pleasure and you harbored a secret resentment against Mama and God for making you give it up. And so you got back at God by preaching atheistical sermons and you got back at Mama by starting to lay young girls.

SHANNON: I have never delivered an atheistical sermon, and never would or could when I go back to the Church.

MAXINE: You're not going back to no Church. Did you mention the charge of statutory rape to the divinity dean?

SHANNON [thrusting his chair back so vehemently that it topples over]: Why don't you let up on me? You haven't let up on me since I got here this morning! Let up on me! Will you please let up on me?

MAXINE [smiling serenely into his rage.]: Aw baby. . . .

SHANNON: What do you mean by "aw baby"? What do you want out of me, Maxine honey?

MAXINE: Just to do this. [She runs her fingers through his hair. He thrusts her hand away.]

SHANNON: Ah, God. [Words fail him. He shakes his head with a slight, helpless laugh and goes down the steps from the verandah.]

MAXINE: The Chinaman in the kitchen says, "No sweat." . . . "No sweat." He says that's all his philosophy. All the Chinese philosophy in three words, "Mei yoo guanchi"—which is Chinese for "No sweat." . . . With your record and a charge of statutory rape hanging over you in Texas, how could you go to a church except to the Holy Rollers with some lively young female rollers and a bushel of hay on the church floor?

SHANNON: I'll drive into town in the bus to post this letter to-night. [*He has started toward the path. There are sounds below. He divides the masking foliage with his hands and looks down the hill.*]

MAXINE [*descending the steps from the verandah*]: Watch out for the spook, he's out there.

SHANNON: My ladies are up to something. They're all down there on the road, around the bus.

MAXINE: They're running out on you, Shannon.

[*She comes up beside him. He draws back and she looks down the hill. The light in number 3 cubicle comes on and Hannah rises from the little table that she had cleared for letter-writing. She removes her Kabuki robe from a hook and puts it on as an actor puts on a costume in his dressing room. Nonno's cubicle is also lighted dimly. He sits on the edge of his cot, rocking slightly back and forth, uttering an indistinguishable mumble of lines from his poem.*]

MAXINE: Yeah. There's a little fat man down there that looks like Jake Latta to me. Yep, that's Jake, that's Latta. I reckon Blake Tours has sent him here to take over your party, Shannon. [*Shannon looks out over the jungle and lights a cigarette with jerky fingers.*] Well, let him do it. No sweat! He's coming up here now. Want me to handle it for you?

SHANNON: I'll handle it for myself. You keep out of it, please.

[*He speaks with a desperate composure. Hannah stands just behind the curtain of her cubicle, motionless as a painted figure, during the scene that follows. Jake Latta comes puffing up the verandah steps, beaming genially.*]

LATTA: Hi there, Larry.

SHANNON: Hello, Jake. [*He folds his letter into an envelope.*] Mrs. Faulk honey, this goes air special.

MAXINE: First you'd better address it.

SHANNON: Oh!

[*Shannon laughs and snatches the letter back, fumbling in his pocket for an address book, his fingers shaking uncontrollably. Latta winks at Maxine. She smiles tolerantly.*]

LATTA: How's our boy doin', Maxine?

MAXINE: He'd feel better if I could get him to take a drink.

LATTA: Can't you get a drink down him?

MAXINE: Nope, not even a rum-coco.

LATTA: Let's have a rum-coco, Larry.

SHANNON: You have a rum-coco, Jake. I have a party of ladies to take care of. And I've discovered that situations come up in this business that call for cold, sober judgment. How about you? Haven't you ever made that discovery, Jake? What're you doing here? Are you here with a party?

LATTA: I'm here to pick up your party, Larry boy.

SHANNON: That's interesting! On whose authority, Jake?

LATTA: Blake Tours wired me in Cuernavaca to pick up your

party here and put them together with mine cause you'd had this little nervous upset of yours and. . . .

SHANNON: Show me the wire! Huh?

LATTA: The bus driver says you took the ignition key to the bus.

SHANNON: That's right. I have the ignition key to the bus and I have this party and neither the bus or the party will pull out of here till I say so.

LATTA: Larry, you're a sick boy. Don't give me trouble.

SHANNON: What jail did they bail you out of, you fat zero?

LATTA: Let's have the bus key, Larry.

SHANNON: Where did they dig you up? You've got no party in Cuernavaca, you haven't been out with a party since 'thirty-seven.

LATTA: Just give me the bus key, Larry.

SHANNON: In a pig's—snout!—like yours!

LATTA: Where is the reverend's bedroom, Mrs. Faulk?

SHANNON: The bus key is in my pocket. [*He slaps his pants pocket fiercely.*] Here, right here, in my pocket! Want it? Try and get it, Fatso!

LATTA: What language for a reverend to use, Mrs. Faulk. . . .

SHANNON [*holding up the key*]: See it? [*He thrusts it back into his pocket.*] Now go back wherever you crawled from. My party of ladies is staying here three more days because several of them are in no condition to travel and neither—neither am I.

LATTA: They're getting in the bus now.

SHANNON: How are you going to start it?

LATTA: Larry, don't make me call the bus driver up here to hold you down while I get that key away from you. You want to see the wire from Blake Tours? Here. [*He produces the wire.*] Read it.

SHANNON: You sent that wire to yourself.

LATTA: From Houston?

SHANNON: You had it sent you from Houston. What's that prove? Why, Blake Tours was nothing, *nothing!*—till they got me. You think they'd let me go?—Ho, ho! Latta, it's caught up with you, Latta, all the whores and tequila have hit your brain now, Latta. [*Latta shouts down the hill for the bus driver.*] Don't you realize what I mean to Blake Tours? Haven't you seen the brochure in which they mention, they brag, that special parties are conducted by the Reverend T. Lawrence Shannon, D.D., noted world traveler, lecturer, son of a minister and grandson of a bishop, and the direct descendant of two colonial governors? [*Miss Fellowes appears at the verandah steps.*] Miss Fellowes has read the brochure, she's memorized the brochure. She knows what it says about me.

MISS FELLOWES [*to Latta*]: Have you got the bus key?

LATTA: Bus driver's going to get it away from him, lady. [*He lights a cigar with dirty, shaky fingers.*]

SHANNON: Ha-ha-ha-ha-ha! [*His laughter shakes him back against the verandah wall.*]

LATTA: He's gone. [*He touches his forehead.*]

SHANNON: Why, those ladies . . . have had . . . some of them, most of them if not all of them . . . for the first time in their lives the advantage of contact, social contact, with a gentleman born and bred, whom under no other circumstances they could have possibly met . . . let alone be given the chance to insult and accuse and. . . .

MISS FELLOWES: Shannon! The girls are in the bus and we want to go now, so give up that key. Now!

[*Hank, the bus driver, appears at the top of the path, whistling casually: he is not noticed at first.*]

SHANNON: If I didn't have a decent sense of responsibility to these parties I take out, I would gladly turn over your party— because I don't like your party—to this degenerate here, this Jake Latta of the gutter-rat Lattas. Yes, I would—I would surrender the bus key in my pocket, even to Latta, but I am not that irresponsible, no, I'm not, to the parties that I take out, regardless of the party's treatment of me. I still feel responsible for them till I get them back wherever I picked them up. [*Hank comes onto the verandah.*] Hi, Hank. Are you friend or foe?

HANK: Larry, I got to get that ignition key now so we can get moving down there.

SHANNON: Oh! Then *foe!* I'm disappointed, Hank. I thought you were friend, not foe. [*Hank puts a wrestler's armlock on Shannon and Latta removes the bus key from his pocket. Hannah raises a hand to her eyes.*] O.K., O.K., you've got the bus key. By force. I feel exonerated now of all responsibility. Take the bus and the ladies in it and go. Hey, Jake, did you know they had Lesbians in Texas—without the dikes the plains of Texas would be engulfed by the Gulf. [*He nods his head violently toward Miss Fellowes, who springs forward and slaps him.*] Thank you, Miss Fellowes. Latta, hold on a minute. I will not be stranded here. I've had unusual expenses on this trip. Right now I don't have my fare back to Houston or even to Mexico City. Now if there's any truth in your statement that Blake Tours have really authorized you to take over my party, then I am sure they have . . . [*He draws a breath, almost gasping.*] . . . I'm sure they must have given you something in the . . . the nature of . . . *severance* pay? Or at least enough to get me back to the States?

LATTA: I got no money for you.

SHANNON: I hate to question your word, but. . . .

LATTA: We'll drive you back to Mexico City. You can sit up front with the driver.

SHANNON: *You* would do that, Latta. *I'd* find it *humiliating.* Now! Give me my severance pay!

LATTA: Blake Tours is having to refund those ladies half the price of the tour. That's your severance pay. And Miss Fellowes tells me you got plenty of money out of this young girl you seduced in. . . .

SHANNON: Miss Fellowes, did you really make such a . . . ?

MISS FELLOWES: When Charlotte returned that night, she'd cashed two traveler's checks.

SHANNON: After I had spent all my own cash.

MISS FELLOWES: On what? Whores in the filthy places you took her through?

SHANNON: Miss Charlotte cashed two ten-dollar traveler's checks because I had spent all the cash I had on me. And I've never had to, I've certainly never desired to, have relations with whores.

MISS FELLOWES: You took her through ghastly places, such as. . . .

SHANNON: I showed her what she wanted me to show her. Ask her! I showed her San Juan de Letran, I showed her Tenampa and some other places not listed in the Blake Tours brochure. I showed her more than the floating gardens at Xochimilco, Maximilian's Palace, and the mad Empress Carlotta's little homesick chapel, Our Lady of Guadalupe, the monument to Juarez, the relics of the Aztec civilization, the sword of Cortez, the headdress of Montezuma. I showed her what she told me she wanted to see. Where is she? Where is Miss . . . oh, down there with the ladies. [*He leans over the rail and shouts down.*] Charlotte! Charlotte! [*Miss Fellowes seizes his arm and thrusts him away from the verandah rail.*]

MISS FELLOWES: Don't you dare!

SHANNON: Dare what?

MISS FELLOWES: Call her, speak to her, go near her, you, you . . . *filthy!*

[*Maxine reappears at the corner of the verandah, with the ceremonial rapidity of a cuckoo bursting from a clock to announce the hour. She just stands there with an incongruous grin, her big eyes unblinking, as if they were painted on her round beaming face. Hannah holds a gold-lacquered Japanese fan motionless but open in one hand; the other hand touches the netting at the cubicle door as if she were checking an impulse to rush to Shannon's defense. Her attitude has the style of a Kabuki dancer's pose. Shannon's manner becomes courtly again.*]

SHANNON: Oh, all right, I won't. I only wanted her to confirm my story that I took her out that night at her request, not at my . . . suggestion. All that I did was offer my services to her when *she* told *me* she'd like to see things not listed in the brochure, not usually witnessed by ordinary tourists such as. . . .

MISS FELLOWES: Your hotel bedroom? Later? That too? She came back *flea*-bitten!

SHANNON: Oh, now, don't exaggerate, please. Nobody ever got any fleas off Shannon.

MISS FELLOWES: Her clothes had to be fumigated!

SHANNON: I understand your annoyance, but you are going too far when you try to make out that I gave Charlotte fleas. I don't deny that. . . .

MISS FELLOWES: Wait till they get my *report!*

SHANNON: I don't deny that it's possible to get fleabites on a tour of inspection of what lies under the public surface of cities, off the grand boulevards, away from the night clubs, even away from Diego Rivera's murals, but. . . .

MISS FELLOWES: Oh, preach that in a pulpit, Reverend Shannon *de*-frocked!

SHANNON [*ominously*]: You've said that once too often. [*He seizes her arm.*] This time before witnesses. Miss Jelkes? Miss Jelkes!

[*Hannah opens the curtain of her cubicle.*]

HANNAH: Yes, Mr. Shannon, what is it?

SHANNON: You heard what this. . . .

MISS FELLOWES: Shannon! Take your hand off my arm!

SHANNON: Miss Jelkes, just tell me, did you hear what she . . . [*His voice stops oddly with a choked sobbing sound. He runs at the wall and pounds it with his fists.*]

MISS FELLOWES: I spent this entire afternoon and over twenty dollars checking up on this impostor, with long-distance phone calls.

HANNAH: Not impostor—you mustn't say things like that.

MISS FELLOWES: You were locked out of your church!—for atheism and seducing of girls!

SHANNON [*turning about*]: In front of God and witnesses, you are lying, lying!

LATTA: Miss Fellowes, I want you to know that Blake Tours was deceived about this character's background and Blake Tours will see that he is blacklisted from now on at every travel agency in the States.

SHANNON: How about Africa, Asia, Australia? The whole world, Latta, God's world, has been the range of my travels. I haven't stuck to the schedules of the brochures and I've always allowed the ones that were willing to see, to *see!*—the underworlds of all places, and if they had hearts to be touched, feelings to feel with, I gave them a priceless chance to feel and be touched. And none will ever forget it, none of them, ever, never! [*The passion of his speech imposes a little stillness.*]

LATTA: Go on, lie back in your hammock, that's all you're good for, Shannon. [*He goes to the top of the path and shouts down the hill.*] O.K., let's get cracking. Get that luggage strapped on top of the bus, we're moving! [*He starts down the hill with Miss Fellowes.*]

NONNO [*incongruously, from his cubicle*]:
> How calmly does the orange branch
> Observe the sky begin to blanch. . . .

[*Shannon sucks in his breath with an abrupt, fierce sound. He rushes off the verandah and down the path toward the road. Hannah calls after him, with a restraining gesture. Maxine appears on the verandah. Then a great commotion commences below the hill, with shrieks of outrage and squeals of shocked laughter.*]

MAXINE [*rushing to the path*]: Shannon! Shannon! Get back up here, get back up here. Pedro, Pancho, traerme a Shannon. Que está haciendo allí? Oh, my God! Stop him, for God's sake, somebody stop him!

[*Shannon returns, panting and spent. He is followed by Maxine.*]

MAXINE: Shannon, go in your room and stay there until that party's gone.

SHANNON: Don't give me orders.

MAXINE: You do what I tell you to do or I'll have you removed—you know where.

SHANNON: Don't push me, don't pull at me, Maxine.

MAXINE: All right, do as I say.

SHANNON: Shannon obeys only Shannon.

MAXINE: You'll sing a different tune if they put you where they put you in 'thirty-six. Remember 'thirty-six, Shannon?

SHANNON: O.K., Maxine, just . . . let me breathe alone, please. I won't go but I will lie in the . . . hammock.

MAXINE: Go into Fred's room where I can watch you.

SHANNON: Later, Maxine, not yet.

MAXINE: Why do you always come here to crack up, Shannon?

SHANNON: It's the hammock, Maxine, the hammock by the rain forest.

MAXINE: Shannon, go in your room and stay there until I get back. Oh, my God, the money. They haven't paid the mother-grabbin' bill. I got to go back down there and collect their goddam bill before they. . . . Pancho, vijilalo, entiendes? [*She rushes back down the hill, shouting "Hey! Just a minute down there!"*]

SHANNON: What did I do? [*He shakes his head, stunned.*] I don't know what I did.

[*Hannah opens the screen of her cubicle but doesn't come out. She is softly lighted so that she looks, again, like a medieval sculpture of a saint. Her pale gold hair catches the soft light. She has let it down and still holds the silver-backed brush with which she was brushing it.*]

SHANNON: God almighty, I . . . what did I do? I don't know what I did. [*He turns to the Mexican boys who have come back up the path.*] Que hice? Que hice?

[*There is breathless, spasmodic laughter from the boys as Pancho informs him that he pissed on the ladies' luggage.*]

PANCHO: Tú measte en las maletas de las señoras!

[*Shannon tries to laugh with the boys, while they bend double with amusement. Shannon's laughter dies out in little choked spasms. Down the hill, Maxine's voice is raised in angry altercation with Jake Latta. Miss Fellowes' voice is lifted and then there is a general rhubarb to which is added the roar of the bus motor.*]

SHANNON: There go my ladies, ha, ha! There go my . . . [*He turns about to meet Hannah's grave, compassionate gaze. He tries to laugh again. She shakes her head with a slight restraining gesture and drops the curtain so that her softly luminous figure is seen as through a mist.*] . . . ladies, the last of my—ha, ha!—ladies. [*He bends far over the verandah rail, then straightens violently and with an animal outcry begins to pull at the chain suspending the gold cross about his neck. Pancho watches indifferently as the chain cuts the back of Shannon's neck. Hannah rushes out to him.*]

HANNAH: Mr. Shannon, stop that! You're cutting yourself doing that. That isn't necessary, so stop it! [*to Pancho:*] Agarrale las manos! [*Pancho makes a halfhearted effort to comply, but Shannon kicks at him and goes on with the furious self-laceration.*] Shannon, let me do it, let me take it off you. Can I take it off you? [*He drops his arms. She struggles with the clasp of the chain but her fingers are too shaky to work it.*]

SHANNON: No, no, it won't come off, I'll have to break it off me.

HANNAH: No, no, wait—I've got it. [*She has now removed it.*]

SHANNON: Thanks. Keep it. Goodbye! [*He starts toward the path down to the beach.*]

HANNAH: Where are you going? What are you going to do?

SHANNON: I'm going swimming. I'm going to swim out to China!

HANNAH: No, no, not tonight, Shannon! Tomorrow . . . tomorrow, Shannon!

[*But he divides the trumpet-flowered bushes and passes through them. Hannah rushes after him, screaming for "Mrs. Faulk." Maxine can be heard shouting for the Mexican boys.*]

MAXINE: Muchachos, cojerlo! Atarlo! Esté loco. Traerlo acqui. Catch him, he's crazy. Bring him back and tie him up!

[*In a few moments Shannon is hauled back through the bushes and onto the verandah by Maxine and the boys. They rope him into the hammock. His struggle is probably not much of a real struggle—histrionics mostly. But Hannah stands wringing her hands by the steps as Shannon, gasping for breath, is tied up.*]

HANNAH: The ropes are too tight on his chest!

MAXINE: No, they're not. He's acting, acting. He likes it! I know this black Irish bastard like nobody ever knowed him, so you keep out of it, honey. He cracks up like this so regular that you can set a calendar by it. Every eighteen months he does it, and twice he's done it here and I've had to pay for his medical care. Now I'm going to call in town to get a doctor to come out here and give him a knockout injection, and if he's not better tomorrow he's going into the Casa de Locos again like he did the last time he cracked up on me!

[*There is a moment of silence.*]

SHANNON: Miss Jelkes?

HANNAH: Yes.

SHANNON: Where are you?

HANNAH: I'm right here behind you. Can I do anything for you?

SHANNON: Sit here where I can see you. Don't stop talking. I have to fight this panic.

[*There is a pause. She moves a chair beside his hammock. The Germans troop up from the beach. They are delighted by the drama that Shannon has provided. In their scanty swimsuits they parade onto the verandah and gather about Shannon's captive figure as if they were looking at a funny animal in a zoo. Their talk is in German except when they speak directly to Shannon or Hannah. Their heavily handsome figures gleam with oily wetness and they keep chuckling lubriciously.*]

HANNAH: Please! Will you be so kind as to leave him alone?

[*They pretend not to understand her. Frau Fahrenkopf bends over Shannon in his hammock and speaks to him loudly and slowly in English.*]

FRAU FAHRENKOPF: Is this true you make pee-pee all over the suitcases of the ladies from Texas? Hah? Hah? You run down there to the bus and right in front of the ladies you pees all over the luggage of the ladies from Texas?

[*Hannah's indignant protest is drowned in the Rabelaisian laughter of the Germans.*]

HERR FAHRENKOPF: Thees is vunderbar, vunderbar! Hah? Thees is a *epic gesture!* Hah? Thees is the way to demonstrate to ladies that you are a American *gentleman!* Hah?

[*He turns to the others and makes a ribald comment. The two women shriek with amusement, Hilda falling back into the arms of Wolfgang, who catches her with his hands over her almost nude breasts.*]

HANNAH [*calling out*]: Mrs. Faulk! Mrs. Faulk! [*She rushes to the verandah angle as Maxine appears there.*] Will you please ask these people to leave him alone. They're tormenting him like an animal in a trap.

[*The Germans are already trooping around the verandah, laughing and capering gaily.*]

SHANNON [*suddenly, in a great shout*]: Regression to infantilism, ha, ha, regression to infantilism . . . The infantile protest, ha, ha, ha, the infantile expression of rage at Mama and rage at God and rage at the goddam crib, and rage at the everything, rage at the . . . everything. . . . Regression to infantilism. . . .

[*Now all have left but Hannah and Shannon.*]

SHANNON: Untie me.

HANNAH: Not yet.

SHANNON: I can't stand being tied up.

HANNAH: You'll have to stand it a while.

SHANNON: It makes me panicky.

HANNAH: I know.

SHANNON: A man can die of panic.

HANNAH: Not if he enjoys it as much as you, Mr. Shannon.

[*She goes into her cubicle directly behind his hammock. The cubicle is lighted and we see her removing a small teapot and a tin of tea from her suitcase on the cot, then a little alcohol burner. She comes back out with these articles.*]

SHANNON: What did you mean by that insulting remark?

HANNAH: What remark, Mr. Shannon?

SHANNON: That I enjoy it.

HANNAH: Oh . . . that.

SHANNON: Yes. That.

HANNAH: That wasn't meant as an insult, just an observation. I don't judge people, I draw them. That's all I do, just draw them, but in order to draw them I have to observe them, don't I?

SHANNON: And you've observed, you think you've observed, that I like being tied in this hammock, trussed up in it like a hog being hauled off to the slaughter house, Miss Jelkes.

HANNAH: Who wouldn't like to suffer and atone for the sins of himself and the world if it could be done in a hammock with ropes instead of nails, on a hill that's so much lovelier than Golgotha, the Place of the Skull, Mr. Shannon? There's something almost voluptuous in the way that you twist and groan in that hammock—no nails, no blood, no death. Isn't that a comparatively comfortable, almost voluptuous kind of crucifixion to suffer for the guilt of the world, Mr. Shannon?

[*She strikes a match to light the alcohol burner. A pure blue jet of flame springs up to cast a flickering, rather unearthly glow on their section of the verandah. The glow is delicately refracted by the subtle, jaded colors of her robe—a robe given to her by a Kabuki actor who posed for her in Japan.*]

SHANNON: Why have you turned against me all of a sudden, when I need you the most?

HANNAH: I haven't turned against you at all, Mr. Shannon. I'm just attempting to give you a character sketch of yourself, in words instead of pastel crayons or charcoal.

SHANNON: You're certainly suddenly very sure of some New England spinsterish attitudes that I didn't know you had in you. I thought that you were an *emancipated* Puritan, Miss Jelkes.

HANNAH: Who is . . . ever . . . completely?

SHANNON: I thought you were sexless but you've suddenly turned into a woman. Know how I know that? Because you, not me—not me—are taking pleasure in my tied-up condition. All women, whether they face it or not, want to see a man in a tied-up situation. They work at it all their lives, to get a man in a tied-up situation. Their lives are fulfilled, they're satisfied at last, when they get a man, or as many men as they can, in the tied-up situation. [*Hannah leaves the alcohol burner and teapot and moves to the railing where she grips a verandah post and draws a few deep breaths.*] You don't like this observation of you? The shoe's too tight for comfort when it's on your own foot, Miss Jelkes? Some deep breaths again—feeling panic?

HANNAH [*recovering and returning to the burner*]: I'd like to untie you right now, but let me wait till you've passed through your present disturbance. You're still indulging yourself in your . . . your Passion Play performance. I can't help observing this self-indulgence in you.

SHANNON: What rotten indulgence?

HANNAH: Well, your busload of ladies from the female college in Texas. I don't like those ladies any more than you do, but after all, they did save up all year to make this Mexican tour, to stay in stuffy hotels and eat the food they're used to. They want to be at home away from home, but you . . . you indulged yourself, Mr. Shannon. You did conduct the tour as if it was just for you, for your own pleasure.

SHANNON: Hell, what pleasure—going through hell all the way?

HANNAH: Yes, but comforted, now and then, weren't you, by the little musical prodigy under the wing of the college vocal instructor?

SHANNON: Funny, ha-ha funny! Nantucket spinsters have their wry humor, don't they?

HANNAH: Yes, they do. They have to.

SHANNON [becoming progressively quieter under the cool influence of her voice behind him]: I can't see what you're up to, Miss Jelkes honey, but I'd almost swear you're making a pot of tea over there.

HANNAH: That is just what I'm doing.

SHANNON: Does this strike you as the right time for a tea party?

HANNAH: This isn't plain tea, this is poppy-seed tea.

SHANNON: Are you a slave to the poppy?

HANNAH: It's a mild, sedative drink that helps you get through nights that are hard for you to get through and I'm making it for my grandfather and myself as well as for you, Mr. Shannon. Because, for all three of us, this won't be an easy night to get through. Can't you hear him in his cell number 4, mumbling over and over and over the lines of his new poem? It's like a blind man climbing a staircase that goes to nowhere, that just falls off into space, and I hate to say what it is. . . . [*She draws a few deep breaths behind him.*]

SHANNON: Put some hemlock in his poppy-seed tea tonight so he won't wake up tomorrow for the removal to the Casa de Huéspedes. Do that act of mercy. Put in the hemlock and I will consecrate it, turn it to God's blood. Hell, if you'll get me out of this hammock I'll serve it to him myself, I'll be your accomplice in this act of mercy. I'll say, "Take and drink this, the blood of our—"

HANNAH: Stop it! Stop being childishly cruel! I can't stand for a person that I respect to talk and behave like a small, cruel boy, Mr. Shannon.

SHANNON: What've you found to respect in me, Miss . . . Thin-Standing-Up-Female-Buddha?

HANNAH: I respect a person that has had to fight and howl for his decency and his—

SHANNON: *What* decency?

HANNAH: Yes, for his decency and his bit of goodness, much more than I respect the lucky ones that just had theirs handed out to them at birth and never afterward snatched away from them by . . . unbearable . . . torments, I. . . .

SHANNON: You *respect* me?

HANNAH: I do.

SHANNON: But you just said that I'm taking pleasure in a . . . voluptuous crucifixion without nails. A . . . what? . . . painless atonement for the—

HANNAH [*cutting in*]: Yes, but I think—

SHANNON: Untie me!

HANNAH: Soon, soon. Be patient.

SHANNON: Now!

HANNAH: Not quite yet, Mr. Shannon. Not till I'm reasonably sure that you won't swim out to China, because, you see, I think you think of the . . . "the long swim to China" as another painless atonement. I mean I don't think you think you'd be intercepted by sharks and barracudas before you got far past the barrier reef. And I'm afraid you *would be*. It's as simple as that, if that is simple.

SHANNON: What's simple?

HANNAH: Nothing, except for simpletons, Mr. Shannon.

SHANNON: Do you believe in people being tied up?

HANNAH: Only when they might take the long swim to China.

SHANNON: All right, Miss Thin-Standing-Up-Female-Buddha, just light a Benson and Hedges cigarette for me and put it in my mouth and take it out when you hear me choking on it—if that doesn't seem to you like another bit of voluptuous self-crucifixion.

HANNAH [*looking about the verandah*]: I will, but . . . where did I put them?

SHANNON: I have a pack of my own in my pocket.

HANNAH: Which pocket?

SHANNON: I don't know which pocket, you'll have to frisk me for it. [*She pats his jacket pocket.*]

HANNAH: They're not in your coat pocket.

SHANNON: Then look for them in my pants' pockets.

[*She hesitates to put her hand in his pants' pockets, for a moment. Hannah has always had a sort of fastidiousness, a reluctance, toward intimate physical contact. But after the momentary fastidious hesitation, she puts her hands in his pants' pocket and draws out the cigarette pack.*]

SHANNON: Now light it for me and put it in my mouth.

[*She complies with these directions. Almost at once he chokes and the cigarette is expelled.*]

HANNAH: You've dropped it on you—where is it?

SHANNON [*twisting and lunging about in the hammock*]: It's under me, under me, burning. Untie me, for God's sake, will you—it's burning me through my pants!

HANNAH: Raise your hips so I can—

SHANNON: I can't, the ropes are too tight. Untie me, untieeeee meeeeee!

HANNAH: I've found it, I've got it!

[*But Shannon's shout has brought Maxine out of her office. She rushes onto the verandah and sits on Shannon's legs.*]

MAXINE: Now hear this, you crazy black Irish mick, you! You Protestant black Irish looney, I've called up Lopez, Doc Lopez. Remember him—the man in the dirty white jacket that come here the last time you cracked up here? And hauled you off to the Casa de Locos? Where they threw you into that cell with nothing in it but a bucket and straw and a water pipe? That you crawled up the water pipe? And dropped head-down on the floor and got a concussion? Yeah, and I told him you were back here to crack up again and if you didn't quiet down here tonight you should be hauled out in the morning.

SHANNON [*cutting in, with the honking sound of a panicky goose*]: Off, off, off, off, off!

HANNAH: Oh, Mrs. Faulk, Mr. Shannon won't quiet down till he's left alone in the hammock.

MAXINE: Then why don't *you* leave him alone?

HANNAH: I'm not sitting on him and he . . . has to be cared for by someone.

MAXINE: And the someone is *you*?

HANNAH: A long time ago, Mrs. Faulk, I had experience with someone in Mr. Shannon's condition, so I know how necessary it is to let them be quiet for a while.

MAXINE: He wasn't quiet, he was shouting.

HANNAH: He will quiet down again. I'm preparing a sedative tea for him, Mrs. Faulk.

MAXINE: Yeah, I see. Put it out. Nobody cooks here but the Chinaman in the kitchen.

HANNAH: This is just a little alcohol burner, a spirit lamp, Mrs. Faulk.

MAXINE: I know what it is. It goes out!

[*She blows out the flame under the burner.*]

SHANNON: Maxine honey? [*He speaks quietly now.*] Stop persecuting this lady. You can't intimidate her. A bitch is no match for a lady except in a brass bed, honey, and sometimes not even there.

[*The Germans are heard shouting for beer—a case of it to take down to the beach.*]

WOLFGANG: Eine Kiste Carta Blanca.

FRAU FAHRENKOPF: Wir haben genug gehabt . . . vielleicht nicht.

HERR FAHRENKOPF: Nein! Niemals genug.

HILDA: Mutter du bist dick . . . aber wir sind es nicht.

SHANNON: Maxine, you're neglecting your duties as a beer-hall waitress. [*His tone is deceptively gentle.*] They want a case of Carta Blanca to carry down to the beach, so give it to 'em . . . and tonight, when the moon's gone down, if you'll let me out of this hammock, I'll try to imagine you as a . . . as a nymph in her teens.

MAXINE: A fat lot of good you'd be in your present condition.

SHANNON: Don't be a sexual snob at your age, honey.

MAXINE: Hah! [*But the unflattering offer has pleased her realistically modest soul, so she goes back to the Germans.*]

SHANNON: Now let me try a bit of your poppy-seed tea, Miss Jelkes.

HANNAH: I ran out of sugar, but I had some ginger, some sugared ginger. [*She pours a cup of tea and sips it.*] Oh, it's not well brewed yet, but try to drink some now and the—[*She lights the burner again.*]—the second cup will be better. [*She crouches by the hammock and presses the cup to his lips. He raises his head to sip it, but he gags and chokes.*]

SHANNON: *Caesar's ghost!*—it could be chased by the witches' brew from Macbeth.

HANNAH: Yes, I know, it's still bitter.

[*The Germans appear on the wing of the verandah and go trooping down to the beach, for a beer festival and a moonlight swim. Even in the relative dark they have a luminous color, an almost phosphorescent pink and gold color of skin. They carry with them a case of Carta Blanca beer and the fantastically painted rubber horse. On their faces are smiles of euphoria as they move like a dream-image, starting to sing a marching song as they go.*]

SHANNON: Fiends out of hell with the . . . voices of . . . angels.

HANNAH: Yes, they call it "the logic of contradictions," Mr. Shannon.

SHANNON [*lunging suddenly forward and undoing the loosened ropes*]: Out! Free! Unassisted!

HANNAH: Yes, I never doubted that you could get loose, Mr. Shannon.

SHANNON: Thanks for your help, anyhow.

HANNAH: Where are you going? [*He has crossed to the liquor cart.*]

SHANNON: Not far. To the liquor cart to make myself a rum-coco.

HANNAH: Oh. . . .

SHANNON [*at the liquor cart*]: Coconut? Check. Machete? Check. Rum? Double check! Ice? The ice-bucket's empty. O.K., it's a night for warm drinks. Miss Jelkes? Would you care to have your complimentary rum-coco?

HANNAH: No thank you, Mr. Shannon.

SHANNON: You don't mind me having mine?

HANNAH: Not at all, Mr. Shannon.

SHANNON: You don't disapprove of this weakness, this self-indulgence?

HANNAH: Liquor isn't your problem, Mr. Shannon.

SHANNON: What is my problem, Mr. Jelkes?

HANNAH: The oldest one in the world—the need to believe in something or in someone—almost anyone—almost anything . . . something.

SHANNON: Your voice sounds hopeless about it.

HANNAH: No, I'm not hopeless about it. In fact, I've discovered something to believe in.

SHANNON: Something like . . . God?

HANNAH: No.

SHANNON: What?

HANNAH: Broken gates between people so they can reach each other, even if it's just for one night only.

SHANNON: One night stands, huh?

HANNAH: One night . . . communication between them on a verandah outside their . . . separate cubicles, Mr. Shannon.

SHANNON: You don't mean physically, do you?

HANNAH: No.

SHANNON: I didn't think so. Then what?

HANNAH: A little understanding exchanged between them, a wanting to help each other through nights like this.

SHANNON: Who was the someone you told the widow you'd helped long ago to get through a crack-up like this one I'm going through?

HANNAH: Oh . . . that. Myself.

SHANNON: You?

HANNAH: Yes. I can help you because I've been through what you are going through now. I had something like your spook— I just had a different name for him. I called him the blue devil, and . . . oh . . . we had quite a battle, quite a contest between us.

SHANNON: Which you obviously won.

HANNAH: I couldn't afford to lose.

SHANNON: How'd you beat your blue devil?

HANNAH: I showed him that I could endure him and I made him respect my endurance.

SHANNON: How?

HANNAH: Just by, just by . . . enduring. Endurance is something that spooks and blue devils respect. And they respect all the tricks that panicky people use to outlast and outwit their panic.

SHANNON: Like poppy-seed tea?

HANNAH: Poppy-seed tea or rum-cocos or just a few deep breaths. Anything, everything, that we take to give them the slip, and so to keep on going.

SHANNON: To where?

HANNAH: To somewhere like this, perhaps. This verandah over the rain forest and the still-water beach, after long, difficult travels. And I don't mean just travels about the world, the earth's surface. I mean . . . subterranean travels, the . . . the journeys that the spooked and bedeviled people are forced to take through the . . . the *unlighted* sides of their natures.

SHANNON: Don't tell me you have a dark side to your nature. [*He says this sardonically.*]

HANNAH: I'm sure I don't have to tell a man as experienced and knowledgeable as you, Mr. Shannon, that everything has its shadowy side?

[*She glances up at him and observes that she doesn't have his attention. He is gazing tensely at something off the verandah. It is the kind of abstraction, not vague but fiercely concentrated, that occurs in madness. She turns to look where he's looking. She closes her eyes for a moment and draws a deep breath, then goes on speaking in a voice like a hypnotist's, as if the words didn't matter, since he is not listening to her so much as to the tone and the cadence of her voice.*]

HANNAH: Everything in the whole solar system has a shadowy side to it except the sun itself—the sun is the single exception. You're not listening, are you?

SHANNON [*as if replying to her*]: The spook is in the rain forest. [*He suddenly hurls his coconut shell with great violence off the verandah, creating a commotion among the jungle birds.*] Good shot—it caught him right on the kisser and his teeth flew out like popcorn from a popper.

HANNAH: Has he gone off—to the dentist?

SHANNON: He's retreated a little way away for a little while, but when I buzz for my breakfast tomorrow, he'll bring it in to me with a grin that'll curdle the milk in the coffee and he'll stink like

113

a . . . a gringo drunk in a Mexican jail who's slept all night in his vomit.

HANNAH: If you wake up before I'm out, I'll bring your coffee in to you . . . if you call me.

SHANNON [*His attention returns to her*]: No, you'll be gone, God help me.

HANNAH: Maybe and maybe not. I might think of something tomorrow to placate the widow.

SHANNON: The widow's implacable, honey.

HANNAH: I think I'll think of something because I have to. I can't let Nonno be moved to the Casa de Huéspedes, Mr. Shannon. Not any more than I could let you take the long swim out to China. You know that. Not if I can prevent it, and when I have to be resourceful, I can be very resourceful.

SHANNON: How'd you get over your crack-up?

HANNAH: I never cracked up, I couldn't afford to. Of course, I nearly did once. I was young once, Mr. Shannon, but I was one of those people who can be young without really having their youth, and not to have your youth when you are young is naturally very disturbing. But I was lucky. My work, this occupational therapy that I gave myself—painting and doing quick character sketches—made me look out of myself, not in, and gradually, at the far end of the tunnel that I was struggling out of I began to see this faint, very faint gray light—the light of the world outside me—and I kept climbing toward it. I had to.

SHANNON: Did it stay a gray light?

HANNAH: No, no, it turned white.

SHANNON: Only white, never gold?

HANNAH: No, it stayed only white, but white is a very good light to see at the end of a long black tunnel you thought would be never-ending, that only God or Death could put a stop to, especially when you . . . since I was . . . far from sure about God.

SHANNON: You're still unsure about him?

HANNAH: Not as unsure as I was. You see, in my profession I have to look hard and close at human faces in order to catch something in them before they get restless and call out, "Waiter, the check, we're leaving." Of course sometimes, a few times, I just see blobs of wet dough that pass for human faces, with bits of jelly for eyes. Then I cue in Nonno to give a recitation, because I can't draw such faces. But those aren't the usual faces, I don't think they're even real. Most times I *do* see something, and I can catch it—I *can*, like I caught something in your face when I sketched you this afternoon with your eyes open. Are you still listening to me? [*He crouches beside her chair, looking up at her intently.*] In Shanghai, Shannon, there is a place that's called the House for the Dying—the old and penniless dying, whose younger, penniless living children and grandchildren take them there for them to get through with their dying on pallets, on straw mats. The first time I went there it shocked me, I ran away from it. But I came back later and I saw that their children and grandchildren and the custodians of the place had put little comforts beside their death-pallets, little flowers and opium candies and religious emblems. That made me able to stay to draw their dying faces. Sometimes only their eyes were still alive, but, Mr. Shannon, those eyes of the penniless dying with those last little comforts beside them, I tell you, Mr. Shannon, those eyes looked up with their last dim life left in them as clear as the stars in the Southern Cross, Mr. Shannon. And now . . . now I am going to say something to you that will sound like something that only the spinster granddaughter of a minor romantic poet is likely to say. . . . Nothing I've ever seen has seemed as beautiful to

115

me, not even the view from this verandah between the sky and the still-water beach, and lately . . . lately my grandfather's eyes have looked up at me like that. . . . [*She rises abruptly and crosses to the front of the verandah.*] Tell me, what is that sound I keep hearing down there?

SHANNON: There's a marimba band at the cantina on the beach.

HANNAH: I don't mean that, I mean that scraping, scuffling sound that I keep hearing under the verandah.

SHANNON: Oh, that. The Mexican boys that work here have caught an iguana and tied it up under the verandah, hitched it to a post, and naturally of course it's trying to scramble away. But it's got to the end of its rope, and get any further it cannot. Ha-ha—that's it. [*He quotes from Nonno's poem:* "And still the orange," *etc.*] Do you have any life of your own—besides your water colors and sketches and your travels with Grampa?

HANNAH: We make a home for each other, my grandfather and I. Do you know what I mean by a home? I don't mean a regular home. I mean I don't mean what other people mean when they speak of a home, because I don't regard a home as a . . . well, as a place, a building . . . a house . . . of wood, bricks, stone. I think of a home as being a thing that two people have between them in which each can . . . well, nest—rest—live in, emotionally speaking. Does that make any sense to you, Mr. Shannon?

SHANNON: Yeah, complete. But. . . .

HANNAH: Another incomplete sentence.

SHANNON: We better leave it that way. I might've said something to hurt you.

HANNAH: I'm not thin skinned, Mr. Shannon.

SHANNON: No, well, then, I'll say it. . . . [*He moves to the liquor cart.*] When a bird builds a nest to rest in and live in, it doesn't build it in a . . . a falling-down tree.

HANNAH: I'm not a bird, Mr. Shannon.

SHANNON: I was making an analogy, Miss Jelkes.

HANNAH: I thought you were making yourself another rum-coco, Mr. Shannon.

SHANNON: Both. When a bird builds a nest, it builds it with an eye for the . . . the relative permanence of the location, and also for the purpose of mating and propagating its species.

HANNAH: I still say that I'm not a bird, Mr. Shannon, I'm a human being and when a member of that fantastic species builds a nest in the heart of another, the question of permanence isn't the first or even the last thing that's considered . . . necessarily? . . . always? Nonno and I have been continually reminded of the impermanence of things lately. We go back to a hotel where we've been many times before and it isn't there any more. It's been demolished and there's one of those glassy, brassy new ones. Or if the old one's still there, the manager or the maître d' who always welcomed us back so cordially before has been replaced by someone new who looks at us with suspicion.

SHANNON: Yeah, but you still had each other.

HANNAH: Yes. We did.

SHANNON: But when the old gentleman goes?

HANNAH: Yes?

SHANNON: What will you do? Stop?

HANNAH: Stop or go on . . . probably go on.

SHANNON: Alone? Checking into hotels alone, eating alone at tables for one in a corner, the tables waiters call aces.

HANNAH: Thank you for your sympathy, Mr. Shannon, but in my profession I'm obliged to make quick contacts with strangers who turn to friends very quickly.

SHANNON: Customers aren't friends.

HANNAH: They turn to friends, if they're friendly.

SHANNON: Yeah, but how will it seem to be traveling alone after so many years of traveling with. . . .

HANNAH: I will know how it feels when I feel it—and don't say alone as if nobody had ever gone on alone. For instance, you.

SHANNON: I've always traveled with trainloads, planeloads and busloads of tourists.

HANNAH: That doesn't mean you're still not really alone.

SHANNON: I never fail to make an intimate connection with someone in my parties.

HANNAH: Yes, the youngest young lady, and I was on the verandah this afternoon when the latest of these young ladies gave a demonstration of how lonely the intimate connection has always been for you. The episode in the cold, inhuman hotel room, Mr. Shannon, for which you despise the lady almost as much as you despise yourself. Afterward you are so polite to the lady that I'm sure it must chill her to the bone, the scrupulous little attentions that you pay her in return for your little enjoyment of her. The gentleman-of-Virginia act that you put on for her, your noblesse oblige treatment of her . . . Oh no, Mr. Shannon, don't kid yourself that you ever travel with someone. You have always traveled alone except for your spook, as you call it.

He's your traveling companion. Nothing, nobody else has traveled with you.

SHANNON: Thank you for your sympathy, Miss Jelkes.

HANNAH: You're welcome, Mr. Shannon. And now I think I had better warm up the poppy-seed tea for Nonno. Only a good night's sleep could make it possible for him to go on from here tomorrow.

SHANNON: Yes, well, if the conversation is over—I think I'll go down for a swim now.

HANNAH: To China?

SHANNON: No, not to China, just to the little island out here with the sleepy bar on it . . . called the Cantina Serena.

HANNAH: Why?

SHANNON: Because I'm not a nice drunk and I was about to ask you a not nice question.

HANNAH: Ask it. There's no set limit on questions here tonight.

SHANNON: And no set limit on answers?

HANNAH: None I can think of between you and me, Mr. Shannon.

SHANNON: That I will take you up on.

HANNAH: Do.

SHANNON: It's a bargain.

HANNAH: Only do lie back down in the hammock and drink a full cup of the poppy-seed tea this time. It's warmer now and the sugared ginger will make it easier to get down.

SHANNON: All right. The question is this: have you never had in your life any kind of a lovelife? [*Hannah stiffens for a moment.*] I thought you said there was no limit set on questions.

HANNAH: We'll make a bargain—I will answer your question *after* you've had a full cup of the poppy-seed tea so you'll be able to get the good night's sleep you need, too. It's fairly warm now and the sugared ginger's made it much more—[*She sips the cup.*]—palatable.

SHANNON: You think I'm going to drift into dreamland so you can welch on the bargain? [*He accepts the cup from her.*]

HANNAH: I'm not a welcher on bargains. Drink it all. All. *All!*

SHANNON [*with a disgusted grimace as he drains the cup*]: Great Caesar's ghost. [*He tosses the cup off the verandah and falls into the hammock, chuckling.*] The Oriental idea of a Mickey Finn, huh? Sit down where I can see you, Miss Jelkes honey. [*She sits down in a straight-back chair, some distance from the hammock.*] Where I can *see* you! I don't have an X-ray eye in the back of my head, Miss Jelkes. [*She moves the chair alongside the hammock.*] Further, further, up further. [*She complies.*] There now. Answer the question now, Miss Jelkes honey.

HANNAH: Would you mind repeating the question.

SHANNON [*slowly, with emphasis*]: Have you never had in all of your life and your travels any experience, any encounter, with what Larry-the-crackpot Shannon thinks of as a lovelife?

HANNAH: There are ... worse things than chastity, Mr. Shannon.

SHANNON: Yeah, lunacy and death are both a little worse, *maybe!* But chastity isn't a thing that a beautiful woman or an attractive man falls into like a booby trap or an overgrown gopher hole, is it? [*There is a pause.*] I still think you are welching on the bargain and I. . . . [*He starts out of the hammock*]

HANNAH: Mr. Shannon, this night is just as hard for me to get through as it is for you to get through. But it's you that are welching on the bargain, you're not staying in the hammock. Lie back down in the hammock. Now. Yes. Yes, I have had two experiences, well, encounters, with. . . .

SHANNON: *Two,* did you say?

HANNAH: Yes, I said two. And I wasn't exaggerating and don't you say "fantastic" before I've told you both stories. When I was sixteen, your favorite age, Mr. Shannon, each Saturday afternoon my grandfather Nonno would give me thirty cents, my allowance, my pay for my secretarial and housekeeping duties. Twenty-five cents for admission to the Saturday matinee at the Nantucket movie theatre and five cents extra for a bag of popcorn, Mr. Shannon. I'd sit at the almost empty back of the movie theatre so that the popcorn munching wouldn't disturb the other movie patrons. Well . . . one afternoon a young man sat down beside me and pushed his . . . knee against mine and . . . I moved over two seats but he moved over beside me and continued this . . . pressure! I jumped up and screamed, Mr. Shannon. He was arrested for molesting a minor.

SHANNON: Is he still in the Nantucket jail?

HANNAH: No. I got him out. I told the police that it was a Clara Bow picture—it *was* a Clara Bow picture—and I was just overexcited.

SHANNON: Fantastic.

HANNAH: Yes, very! The second experience is much more recent, only two years ago, when Nonno and I were operating at the Raffles Hotel in Singapore, and doing very well there, making expenses and more. One evening in the Palm Court of the Raffles we met this middle-aged, sort of nondescript Australian salesman. You know—plump, bald-spotted, with a bad attempt at speaking with an upper-class accent and terribly overfriendly. He was alone and looked lonely. Grandfather said him a poem and I did a quick character sketch that was shamelessly flattering of him. He paid me more than my usual asking price and gave my grandfather five Malayan dollars, yes, and he even purchased one of my water colors. Then it was Nonno's bedtime. The Aussie salesman asked me out in a sampan with him. Well, he'd been so generous . . . I accepted. I did, I accepted. Grandfather went up to bed and I went out in the sampan with this ladies' underwear salesman. I noticed that he became more and more. . . .

SHANNON: What?

HANNAH: Well . . . *agitated* . . . as the afterglow of the sunset faded out on the water. [*She laughs with a delicate sadness.*] Well, finally, eventually, he leaned toward me . . . we were vis-à-vis in the sampan . . . and he looked intensely, passionately into my eyes. [*She laughs again.*] And he said to me: "Miss Jelkes? Will you do me a favor? Will you do something for me?" "What?" said I. "Well," said he, "if I turn my back, if I look the other way, will you take off some piece of your clothes and let me hold it, just hold it?"

SHANNON: Fantastic!

HANNAH: Then he said, "It will just take a few seconds." "Just a few seconds for what?" I asked him. [*She gives the same laugh again.*] He didn't say for what, but. . . .

SHANNON: His satisfaction?

HANNAH: Yes.

SHANNON: What did you do—in a situation like that?

HANNAH: I . . . gratified his request, I did! And he kept his promise. He did keep his back turned till I said ready and threw him . . . the part of my clothes.

SHANNON: What did he do with it?

HANNAH: He didn't move, except to seize the article he'd requested. I looked the other way while his satisfaction took place.

SHANNON: Watch out for commercial travelers in the Far East. Is that the moral, Miss Jelkes honey?

HANNAH: Oh, no, the moral is Oriental. Accept whatever situation you cannot improve.

SHANNON: "When it's inevitable, lean back and enjoy it—is that it?

HANNAH: He'd bought a water color. The incident was embarrassing, not violent. I left and returned unmolested. Oh, and the funniest part of all is that when we got back to the Raffles Hotel, he took the piece of apparel out of his pocket like a bashful boy producing an apple for his schoolteacher and tried to slip it into my hand in the elevator. I wouldn't accept it. I whispered, "Oh, please keep it, Mr. Willoughby!" He'd paid the asking price for my water color and somehow the little experience had been rather touching, I mean it was so *lonely,* out there in the sampan with violet streaks in the sky and this little middle-aged Australian making sounds like he was dying of asthma! And the planet Venus coming serenely out of a fair-weather cloud, over the Strait of Malacca. . . .

SHANNON: And that experience . . . you call that a. . . .

HANNAH: A love experience? Yes. I do call it one.

[*He regards her with incredulity, peering into her face so closely that she is embarrassed and becomes defensive.*]

SHANNON: That, that . . . sad, dirty little episode, you call it a . . . ?

HANNAH [*cutting in sharply*]: Sad it certainly was—for the odd little man—but why do you call it "dirty"?

SHANNON: How did you feel when you went into your bedroom?

HANNAH: Confused, I . . . a little confused, I suppose. . . . I'd known about loneliness—but not that degree or . . . depth of it.

SHANNON: You mean it didn't *disgust* you?

HANNAH: Nothing human disgusts me unless it's unkind, violent. And I told you how gentle he was—apologetic, shy, and really very, well, *delicate* about it. However, I do grant you it was on the rather fantastic level.

SHANNON: You're. . . .

HANNAH: I am *what?* "Fantastic"?

[*While they have been talking, Nonno's voice has been heard now and then, mumbling, from his cubicle. Suddenly it becomes loud and clear.*]

NONNO:

And finally the broken stem,
The plummeting to earth and then. . . .

[*His voice subsides to its mumble. Shannon, standing behind Hannah, places his hand on her throat.*]

HANNAH: What is that for? Are you about to strangle me, Mr. Shannon?

SHANNON: You can't stand to be touched?

HANNAH: Save it for the widow. It isn't for me.

SHANNON: Yes, you're right. [*He removes his hand.*] I could do it with Mrs. Faulk, the inconsolable widow, but I couldn't with you.

HANNAH [*dryly and lightly*]: Spinster's loss, widow's gain, Mr. Shannon.

SHANNON: Or widow's loss, spinster's gain. Anyhow it sounds like some old parlor game in a Virginia or Nantucket Island parlor. But . . . I wonder something. . . .

HANNAH: What do you wonder?

SHANNON: If we couldn't . . . *travel* together, I mean just *travel* together?

HANNAH: Could we? In your opinion?

SHANNON: Why not, I don't see why not.

HANNAH: I think the impracticality of the idea will appear much clearer to you in the morning, Mr. Shannon. [*She folds her dimly gold-lacquered fan and rises from her chair.*] Morning can always be counted on to bring us back to a more realistic level. . . . Good night, Mr. Shannon. I have to pack before I'm too tired to.

SHANNON: Don't leave me out here alone yet.

HANNAH: I have to pack now so I can get up at daybreak and try my luck in the plaza.

SHANNON: You won't sell a water color or sketch in that blazing hot plaza tomorrow. Miss Jelkes honey, I don't think you're operating on the realistic level.

125

HANNAH: Would I be if I thought we could travel together?

SHANNON: I still don't see why we couldn't.

HANNAH: Mr. Shannon, you're not well enough to travel any-where with anybody right now. Does that sound cruel of me?

SHANNON: You mean that I'm stuck here for good? Winding up with the . . . inconsolable widow?

HANNAH: We all wind up with something or with someone, and if it's someone instead of just something, we're lucky, perhaps . . . unusually lucky. [*She starts to enter her cubicle, then turns to him again in the doorway.*] Oh, and tomorrow. . . . [*She touches her forehead as if a little confused as well as exhausted.*]

SHANNON: What about tomorrow?

HANNAH [*with difficulty*]: I think it might be better, tomorrow, if we avoid showing any particular interest in each other, because Mrs. Faulk is a morbidly jealous woman.

SHANNON: *Is she?*

HANNAH: Yes, she seems to have misunderstood our . . . sym-pathetic interest in each other. So I think we'd better avoid any more long talks on the verandah. I mean till she's thoroughly reas-sured it might be better if we just say good morning or good night to each other.

SHANNON: We don't even have to say that.

HANNAH: I will, but you don't have to answer.

SHANNON [*savagely*]: How about wall-tappings between us by way of communication? You know, like convicts in separate cells communicate with each other by tapping on the walls of the cells? One tap: I'm here. Two taps: are you there? Three taps: yes, I am.

Four taps: that's good, we're together. *Christ!* . . . Here, take this. [*He snatches the gold cross from his pocket.*] Take my gold cross and hock it, it's 22-carat gold.

HANNAH: What do you, what are you . . . ?

SHANNON: There's a fine amethyst in it, it'll pay your travel expenses back to the States.

HANNAH: Mr. Shannon, you're making no sense at all now.

SHANNON: Neither are you, Miss Jelkes, talking about tomorrow, and. . . .

HANNAH: All I was saying was. . . .

SHANNON: You won't *be* here tomorrow! Had you forgotten you won't be here tomorrow?

HANNAH [*with a slight, shocked laugh*]: Yes, I *had,* I'd *forgotten!*

SHANNON: The widow wants you out and out you'll go, even if you sell your water colors like hotcakes to the pariah dogs in the plaza. [*He stares at her, shaking his head hopelessly.*]

HANNAH: I suppose you're right, Mr. Shannon. I must be too tired to think or I've contracted your fever. . . . It had actually slipped my mind for a moment that—

NONNO [*abruptly, from his cubicle*]: Hannah!

HANNAH [*rushing to his door*]: Yes, what is it, Nonno? [*He doesn't hear her and repeats her name louder.*] Here I am, I'm here.

NONNO: Don't come in yet, but stay where I can call you.

HANNAH: Yes, I'll *hear* you, Nonno. [*She turns toward Shannon, drawing a deep breath.*]

SHANNON: Listen, if you don't take this gold cross that I never want on me again, I'm going to pitch it off the verandah at the spook in the rain forest. [*He raises an arm to throw it, but she catches his arm to restrain him.*]

HANNAH: All right, Mr. Shannon, I'll take it, I'll hold it for you.

SHANNON: Hock it, honey, you've got to.

HANNAH: Well, if I do, I'll mail the pawn ticket to you so you can redeem it, because you'll want it again, when you've gotten over your fever. [*She moves blindly down the verandah and starts to enter the wrong cubicle.*]

SHANNON: That isn't your cell, you went past it. [*His voice is gentle again.*]

HANNAH: I did, I'm sorry. I've never been this tired in all my life. [*She turns to face him again. He stares into her face. She looks blindly out, past him.*] Never! [*There is a slight pause.*] What did you say is making that constant, dry, scuffling sound beneath the verandah?

SHANNON: I told you.

HANNAH: I didn't hear you.

SHANNON: I'll get my flashlight, I'll show you. [*He lurches rapidly into his cubicle and back out with a flashlight.*] It's an iguana. I'll show you. . . . See? The iguana? At the end of its rope? Trying to go on past the end of its goddam rope? Like *you!* Like *me!* Like Grampa with his last poem!

[*In the pause which follows singing is heard from the beach.*]

HANNAH: What is a—what—iguana?

SHANNON: It's a kind of lizard—a big one, a giant one. The Mexican kids caught it and tied it up.

HANNAH: Why did they tie it up?

SHANNON: Because that's what they do. They tie them up and fatten them up and then eat them up, when they're ready for eating. They're a delicacy. Taste like white meat of chicken. At least the Mexicans think so. And also the kids, the Mexican kids, have a lot of fun with them, poking out their eyes with sticks and burning their tails with matches. You know? Fun? Like that?

HANNAH: Mr. Shannon, please go down and cut it loose!

SHANNON: I can't do that.

HANNAH: Why can't you?

SHANNON: Mrs. Faulk wants to eat it. I've got to please Mrs. Faulk, I am at her mercy. I am at her disposal.

HANNAH: I don't understand. I mean I don't understand how anyone could eat a big lizard.

SHANNON: Don't be so critical. If you got hungry enough you'd eat it too. You'd be surprised what people will eat if hungry. There's a lot of hungry people still in the world. Many have died of starvation, but a lot are still living and hungry, believe you me, if you will take my word for it. Why, when I was conducting a party of—*ladies?*—yes, ladies . . . through a country that shall be nameless but in this world, we were passing by rubberneck bus along a tropical coast when we saw a great mound of . . . well, the smell was unpleasant. One of my ladies said, "Oh, Larry, what is that?" My name being Lawrence, the most familiar ladies sometimes call me Larry. I didn't use the four letter word for what the great mound was. I didn't think it was necessary to say it. Then she noticed, and I noticed too, a pair of very old natives of this nameless country, practically naked except for a few filthy rags, creeping and crawling about this mound of . . . and . . . occasionally stopping to pick something out of it, and pop it into their mouths. What? Bits of undigested . . . food particles, Miss Jelkes. [*There is silence for a moment. She makes a gagging sound in her throat and rushes the length of the verandah to the wooden steps and disappears for a while. Shannon continues, to himself and the moon.*] Now why did I tell her that? Because it's true? That's no reason to tell her, because it's true. Yeah. Because it's true was a good reason not to tell her. Except . . . I think I first *faced* it in that nameless country. The gradual, rapid, natural, unnatural—predestined, accidental—cracking up and going to pieces of young Mr. T. Lawrence Shannon, yes, still *young* Mr. T. Lawrence Shannon, by which rapid-slow process . . . his final tour of ladies through tropical countries. . . . Why did I say "tropical"? Hell! Yes! It's always been tropical countries I took ladies through. Does that, does that—huh?—signify something, I wonder? Maybe. Fast decay is a thing of hot climates, steamy, hot, wet climates, and I run back to them like a. . . . Incomplete sentence. . . . Always seducing a lady or two, or three or four or five ladies in the party, but really ravaging her first by pointing out to her the—what?—horrors? Yes, horrors!—of the tropical country being conducted a tour through. My . . . brain's going out now, like a failing—power. . . . So I stay here, I reckon, and live off la patrona for the rest of my life. Well, she's old enough to predecease me. She could check out of here first, and I imagine that after a couple of years of having to satisfy her I might be prepared for the shock of her passing on. . . . Cruelty . . . pity. What is it? . . . Don't know, all I know is. . . .

HANNAH: [*from below the verandah*]: You're talking to yourself.

SHANNON: No. To you. I knew you could hear me out there, but not being able to see you I could say it easier, you know . . . ?

NONNO:

> A chronicle no longer gold,
> A bargaining with mist and mould. . . .

HANNAH [*coming back onto the verandah*]: I took a closer look at the iguana down there.

SHANNON: You did? How did you like it? Charming? Attractive?

HANNAH: No, it's not an attractive creature. Nevertheless I think it should be cut loose.

SHANNON: Iguanas have been known to bite their tails off when they're tied up by their tails.

HANNAH: This one is tied by its throat. It can't bite its own head off to escape from the end of the rope, Mr. Shannon. Can you look at me and tell me truthfully that you don't know it's able to feel pain and panic?

SHANNON: You mean it's one of God's creatures?

HANNAH: If you want to put it that way, yes, it is. Mr. Shannon, will you please cut it loose, set it free? Because if you don't, I will.

SHANNON: Can you look at *me* and tell *me* truthfully that this reptilian creature, tied up down there, doesn't mostly disturb you because of its parallel situation to your Grampa's dying-out effort to finish one last poem, Miss Jelkes?

HANNAH: Yes, I. . . .

SHANNON: Never mind completing that sentence. We'll play God tonight like kids play house with old broken crates and boxes. All right? Now Shannon is going to go down there with his machete and cut the damn lizard loose so it can run back to its bushes because God won't do it and we are going to play God here.

HANNAH: I knew you'd do that. And I thank you.

[*Shannon goes down the two steps from the verandah with the machete. He crouches beside the cactus that hides the iguana and cuts the rope with a quick, hard stroke of the machete. He turns to look after its flight, as the low, excited mumble in cubicle 3 grows louder. Then Nonno's voice turns to a sudden shout.*]

NONNO: *Hannah! Hannah!* [*She rushes to him, as he wheels himself out of his cubicle onto the verandah.*]

HANNAH: Grandfather! What is it?

NONNO: I! believe! it! is! *finished!* Quick, before I forget it—pencil, paper! Quick! please! Ready?

HANNAH: Yes. All ready, Grandfather.

NONNO [*in a loud, exalted voice*]:

> How calmly does the orange branch
> Observe the sky begin to blanch
> Without a cry, without a prayer,
> With no betrayal of despair.
>
> Sometime while night obscures the tree
> The zenith of its life will be
> Gone past forever, and from thence
> A second history will commence.
>
> A chronicle no longer gold,
> A bargaining with mist and mould,
> And finally the broken stem
> The plummeting to earth; and then
>
> An intercourse not well designed
> For beings of a golden kind

Whose native green must arch above
The earth's obscene, corrupting love.

And still the ripe fruit and the branch
Observe the sky begin to blanch
Without a cry, without a prayer,
With no betrayal of despair.

O Courage, could you not as well
Select a second place to dwell,
Not only in that golden tree
But in the frightened heart of me?

Have you got it?

HANNAH: Yes!

NONNO: All of it?

HANNAH: Every word of it.

NONNO: It is *finished?*

HANNAH: Yes.

NONNO: Oh! God! Finally finished?

HANNAH: Yes, finally finished. [*She is crying. The singing voices flow up from the beach.*]

NONNO: After waiting so long!

HANNAH: Yes, we waited so long.

NONNO: And it's good! It is *good?*

HANNAH: It's—it's. . . .

NONNO: What?

HANNAH: Beautiful, Grandfather! [*She springs up, a fist to her mouth.*] Oh, Grandfather, I am so happy for you. Thank you for writing such a lovely poem! It was worth the long wait. Can you sleep now, Grandfather?

NONNO: You'll have it typewritten tomorrow?

HANNAH: Yes. I'll have it typed up and send it off to *Harper's*.

NONNO: Hah? I didn't hear that, Hannah.

HANNAH [*shouting*]: I'll have it typed up tomorrow, and mail it to *Harper's* tomorrow! They've been waiting for it a long time, too! You know!

NONNO: Yes, I'd like to pray now.

HANNAH: Good night. Sleep now, Grandfather. You've finished your loveliest poem.

NONNO [*faintly, drifting off*]: Yes, thanks and praise . . .

[*Maxine comes around the front of the verandah, followed by Pedro playing a harmonica softly. She is prepared for a night swim, a vividly striped towel thrown over her shoulders. It is apparent that the night's progress has mellowed her spirit: her face wears a faint smile which is suggestive of those cool, impersonal, all-comprehending smiles on the carved heads of Egyptian or Oriental dieties. Bearing a rum-coco, she approaches the hammock, discovers it empty, the ropes on the floor, and calls softly to Pedro.*]

MAXINE: Shannon ha escapade! [*Pedro goes on playing dreamily. She throws back her head and shouts.*] SHANNON! [*The call is echoed by the hill beyond. Pedro advances a few steps and points under the verandah.*]

PEDRO: Miré. Allé 'hasta Shannon.

[*Shannon comes into view from below the verandah, the severed rope and machete dangling from his hands.*]

MAXINE: What are you doing down there, Shannon?

SHANNON: I cut loose one of God's creatures at the end of the rope.

[*Hannah, who has stood motionless with closed eyes behind the wicker chair, goes quietly toward the cubicles and out of the moon's glare.*]

MAXINE [*tolerantly*]: What'd you do that for, Shannon.

SHANNON: So that one of God's creatures could scramble home safe and free. . . . A little act of grace, Maxine.

MAXINE [*smiling a bit more definitely*]: C'mon up here, Shannon. I want to talk to you.

SHANNON [*starting to climb onto the verandah, as Maxine rattles the ice in the coconut shell*]: What d'ya want to talk about, Widow Faulk?

MAXINE: Let's go down and swim in that liquid moonlight.

SHANNON: Where did you pick up that poetic expression?

[*Maxine glances back at Pedro and dismisses him with, "Vamos." He leaves with a shrug, the harmonica fading out.*]

MAXINE: Shannon, I want you to stay with me.

SHANNON [*taking the rum-coco from her*]: You want a drinking companion?

MAXINE: No, I just want you to stay here, because I'm alone here now and I need somebody to help me manage the place.

[*Hannah strikes a match for a cigarette.*]

SHANNON [*looking toward her*]: I want to remember that face. I won't see it again.

MAXINE: Let's go down to the beach.

SHANNON: I can make it down the hill, but not back up.

MAXINE: I'll get you back up the hill. [*They have started off now, toward the path down through the rain forest.*] I've got five more years, maybe ten, to make this place attractive to the male clientele, the middle-aged ones at least. And you can take care of the women that are with them. That's what you can do, you know that, Shannon.

[*He chuckles happily. They are now on the path, Maxine half leading half supporting him. Their voices fade as Hannah goes into Nonno's cubicle and comes back with a shawl, her cigarette left inside. She pauses between the door and the wicker chair and speaks to herself and the sky.*]

HANNAH: Oh, God, can't we stop now? Finally? Please let us. It's so quiet here, now.

[*She starts to put the shawl about Nonno, but at the same moment his head drops to the side. With a soft intake of breath, she extends a hand before his mouth to see if he is still breathing. He isn't. In a panicky moment, she looks right and left for someone to call to. There's no one. Then she bends to press her head to the crown of Nonno's and the curtain starts to descend.*]

THE END

Nazi Marching Song

Heute wollen wir ein Liedlein singen,
Trinken wollen wir den kuehlen Wein;
Und die Glaeser sollen dazu klingen,
Denn es muss, es muss geschieden sein.

Gib' mir deine Hand,
Deine weisse Hand,
Leb'wohl, mein Schatz, leb'wohl, mein Schatz
Lebe wohl, lebe wohl,
Denn wir fahren. Boom! Boom!
Denn wir fahren. Boom! Boom!
Denn wir fahren gegen Engelland. Boom! Boom!

Let's sing a little song today,
And drink some cool wine;
The glasses should be ringing
Since we must, we must part.

Give me your hand,
Your white hand,
Farewell, my love, farewell,
Farewell, farewell,
Since we're going—
Since we're going—
Since we're going against England.

ACTS OF GRACE

Tennessee Williams knew well that memory can be a ponderous burden, a tie that shackles the individual to a past from which he or she would perhaps love to escape, but that paradoxically, memory can be a blessing, a prop sustaining one during hard times. Among the treasured memories that bolster me is one of a bitterly cold, snowy evening in Chicago when I experienced perhaps the most remarkable epiphany in theater that I have ever known. I had driven to Chicago in 1961 from Memphis, where I was teaching, for a two-fold purpose: to visit friends and to see the out-of-town premiere of Williams's latest play, *The Night of the Iguana*. I had come to love the plays of Williams not only through my connection to him as a Southerner, Mississippi-born as I was, but also through my love of English Romantic poetry, for in those works was to be found the roots of much of the dramatist's philosophy and method.

Nothing had prepared this life-long resident of the Deep South for the bitter chill of that Midwest City which was, unknown to me, on the verge of a real blizzard. As we walked from the parking lot to the Blackstone Theatre, we were very near Lake Michigan, and the wind whipping around us was sharply brutal. The warmth of the theater lobby was more than welcome, mixed with the excitement of being present at the birth of a new Williams work, an unknown play, waiting in the wings to astound.

The cast of that original production was perhaps as fine as any that has been assembled for *The Night of the Iguana*. Bette Davis, who had been performing mostly in movies for a number of years and thus had an unfortunate tendency to look out into the audience when she was "off camera," nevertheless embodied the earthiness of Maxine, described by Williams as "affable and rapaciously lusty." Patrick O'Neal was certainly effective as Shannon although he did not bring to the role the appropriate near-madness that is evident in Richard Burton's portrayal in the movie. And Alan Webb was a touching Nonno, exhibiting the humor and pathos that are components of the old poet's character.

Not surprisingly, however, it was Margaret Leighton, who performed most memorably in her luminous creation of Hannah—the kind of woman Tennessee may have believed his sister Rose might have been had her life not been wrenched out of shape by mental disorder and the draconian method employed to control it. The playwright needed and would surely have welcomed such a calming and centered woman as a companion, a benefit he seems to have been denied, surrounded as he was by his "dragon ladies," as he dubbed many of his female friends. Only a few years before his death, Tennessee declared Hannah Jelkes "the greatest female character I ever created." Hannah is also the calm, comforting force that Blanche DuBois and Alma Winemiller might have been, had they been freed of the pressure of their psychological dysfunctions.

That night I left the theater changed, having experienced that powerful *Katharsis* about which Aristotle wrote. I had been swept up completely in the action of the play and felt, as I had when, as a child, I would spend most of an afternoon in a darkened movie theater and walk out into the shock of the sunshiny world. Early the next morning, as I drove south, fleeing the snow that was transforming everything in sight, I knew that I had witnessed a theatrical miracle. I have seen many great performances in many great plays since that night, and a number of them have been unforgettable—Cherry Jones as Hannah, for example, Annalee Jefferies as Blanche DuBois, and Zoe Caldwell as Maria Callas in *Master Class*—but that Chicago *Iguana*, with Margaret Leighton's Hannah remains the touchstone of all my theater experiences.

The Night of the Iguana was to be Tennessee Williams's last critical success in the theater. When I announce that it is my favorite of his plays, I am as often as not greeted with surprised looks and the inevitable question: why? The reason is a simple one. A play is an olio of words, ideas, characters, plot, setting, and design, and *Iguana* has all of those in perfected form. Tennessee was engaged most of his life in the struggle between the faith of his childhood and the growing skepticism brought on by the vicissitudes of life. With this play the answer seems finally to have come, so that like Hannah, although he has been "far from sure about God," at this point he is no longer "as unsure as I was." When I asked the late Cleanth Brooks what his favorite work of Faulkner was, he replied without hesitation, "*Absalom, Absalom!* Because it has more of Faulkner in it than any of the others." For me, the same is true of *The Night of the Iguana*; the life of Tennessee Williams is embodied in this play far beyond what can be termed "autobiographical."

In the short story of the same name that preceded *The Night of the Iguana*, one autobiographical element of the play is made clear. A character named Edith Jelkes, is described as a member of "an historical Southern family of great but now moribund vitality," a reflection of the playwright's descent from several prominent Tennessee ancestors. Edith's family, we are told in the story, were "turbulently split" into two groups, one with over-active libidos, the other almost lacking in passion Among them was an abundance of "nervous talents and sickness, of drunkards and poets, gifted artists and sexual degenerates, together with fanatically proper and squeamish old ladies of both sexes who were condemned to live beneath the same roof with relatives whom they could only regard as monsters." One can only imagine the perhaps perverse pleasure with which Williams penned that passage in the short story, reflecting upon his own family with a somewhat jaundiced humor.

The setting in which the characters in great plays gather to act our their life dramas is often a confined space: the home of George and Martha in Albee's *Who's Afraid of Virginia Woolf*, for example, or the "Hell" of Jean-Paul Sartre's *No Exit*. Tennessee excelled in creating the claustrophobic locale; the Wingfield's cramped St. Louis apartment in *Menagerie* or the French Quarter apartment of *Streetcar*. In *The Night of the Iguana*, the hill on which the hotel is located evokes mythological and Biblical mountains on which enlightenment may come or where sacrifices are made. Taken in the latter sense, it is compared by Hannah to the hill on which Christ was executed, when she observes that Shannon's crucifixion while tied up in the hammock takes place "on a hill so much lovelier than Golgotha, the Place of the Skull."

The characters of the play, most of whom are "at the end of their rope," are perhaps more trustworthy when talking about themselves than some of those in *Streetcar* or *Menagerie*; Blanche and Amanda both tell the truth sometimes, but "tell it slant." Shannon and Hannah—note the similarities of the names—have both spent their lives in a search for the truth, although they have chosen different paths to this dark night of the soul. Shannon, despite his past, considers himself a gentleman, as he repeatedly reminds Miss Fellows, and he tells Hannah that she is "a lady, a real one and a great one." Shannon is haunted by a spook much in the same way Hannah endures her "blue devils." Both feel the strong need to believe in "something or in someone."

Tennessee described Maxine, the third major character, in a note to Bette Davis during rehearsals: "Everything about her should have the openness and freedom of the sea. . . . She's the living definition of nature . . . She moves with the ease of clouds and the tides." The widow Maxine, though untroubled and even unaware of the philosophical questions that concern Shannon and Hannah, is nevertheless vulnerable and searching for human connections. In the character of Nonno, Tennessee pays tribute to his beloved grandfather, Rev. Walter Dakin, who had died in 1955 at the age of ninety-seven. Nonno's full name is Jonathan Coffin, the surname taken from Williams's own New England family line. Other characters, including the teenaged temptress Charlotte and her "guardian," Judith Fellowes, and the four obnoxiously healthy German tourists exulting in the firebombing of London on the other side of the world represent, in existential terms, those who according to Kierkegaard are in deepest despair because they do not realizes that they are in despair at all.

The Night of the Iguana reveals a change in religious and philosophical attitudes from the naturalistic world-view found in *Streetcar* and *Summer and Smoke*, to an almost eastern serenity and acceptance. In *Streetcar*, flesh wins the battle against spirit, as Stella "hang[s] back with the brutes," and in *Summer and Smoke* Alma is unable to effect a balance between the demands of body and soul and so moves toward a world of physical abandon. But in *The Night of the Iguana*, a balance seems to be achieved through the good and graceful ministry of Hannah, who has pulled herself up by sheer force of will into a realm in which she can still empathize with and aid those struggling with the material. (Shannon refers to her as "Miss Thin-Standing-Up-Female-Buddha.") There is no longer the brutality, the deliberate cruelty of Stanley and others, except as exhibited by the Mexican youths toward the iguana and the rather abstract cruelty exhibited by the Germans ("Fiends out of Hell," Shannon calls them, "with the . . . voices . . . of angels.")

It would be difficult to over-emphasize the abiding influence of his Southern Protestant upbringing, with its emphasis on reading the sonorous prose and poetry of the King James Bible and singing the equally literary hymns, on Tom Williams the boy, and on the playwright he became. This religious influence was a fact that he continued to assert unabashedly in a world in which less and less credence was given to belief by the literary and theatrical circles in which he moved. But he was a Southerner, and from the Deep South at that, where, Alfred Kazin observed, Protestants "did not deal in pale abstract words only on Sunday but in the reality of the deity and man's relation to Him." Rick Bragg observed in a *New York Times* article on Willie Morris's funeral that the service had a very religious tone, "this being Mississippi, where people talk about God without feeling funny about it." Tennessee continued to refer to himself throughout his adult life as a "puritan," even when his actions might have suggested otherwise, and he made no attempt to hide his abiding faith from his friends. Nowhere is the religious component of the playwright's life more evident than in *The Night of the Iguana.*

How does this involvement with faith manifest itself in Tennessee's dramas? As a student at the University of Iowa, he would have been well aware of the development theater history from ancient Greece to Rome to medieval Europe to the later flowering of playwrights and plays in twentieth century America. He was aware of the significance of such dramatic genres as mystery, miracle, and passion plays, and through his family, he would have become acquainted with the *The Divine Comedy, Paradise Lost,* and allegorical works such as John Bunyan's *Pilgrim's Progress.* Late in life, he told a theater director who was dramatizing Pilgrim's Progress that it had been "the single most important influence on my work." Even given Williams's tendency to exaggerate, one must assume that there is some truth in the assertion.

In the *Oxford English Dictionary,* grace is defined in numerous ways, but the one most pertinent here is "The divine influence which operates in men to regenerate and sanctify, to inspire virtuous impulses, and to impart strength to endure trial and resist temptation." However, it is also defined as "the free and unmerited favor of God," which may be that "amazing grace," which some Christians believe "can save a wretch like me." Being in "a state of grace" is being "under divine influence," and "fallen from grace" is the state of having lost the connection to God. In Williams's hands, grace is the ability to endure life, no matter how appalling, a quality exemplified in the lives and actions of Hannah and her grandfather. Hannah, with her "delicate sadness," has supported her ninety-seven-year-old grandfather in their seemingly endless travel around the world, when it would have been simpler to remain in Nantucket where friends and perhaps surviving family might offer support. She has done what the old poet wanted in order to make his life richer, and that is part of her grace.

Hannah is a peacemaker, much like Tennessee's grandmother, Rose Dakin, who during the turbulent family years in St. Louis, came to visit, bringing with her grace from the deep South. Hannah's grace is simple and without ostentation, but she recognizes in Shannon a desire for grace that coexists with self-indulgence. Struggling to free himself, he complains, "A man can die of panic," and Hannah replies that he enjoys his "Passion Play performance" that occurs "in a hammock with ropes instead of nails . . ." In contrast to his "almost voluptuous kind of crucifixion," Hannah, who is surely just as beset as Shannon, suffers in silence and seems to have achieved that peace St. Paul describes, "which passeth understanding."

The Night of the Iguana is deeply involved in the nature of God, but there are other themes and motifs at work here as well. It is not surprising that Hannah, as the moral center of the play, is the speaker who voices most of these. She defines "home" as "a thing that two people have between them in which each can . . . well, nest—rest—live in, emotionally speaking." She believes that "We all wind up with something or with someone, and if it's someone instead of just something, we're lucky...." She believes in accepting "whatever situation you cannot improve" and, like Blanche DuBois insists that "Nothing human disgusts me unless it's unkind, violent." The epigraph to the play is an Emily Dickinson quatrain from the poem "I Died for Beauty," in which two souls rest in adjacent tombs, one of whom died for beauty, the other for truth:

> And so, as kinsmen met a night,
> We talked between the rooms,
> Until the moss had reached our lips,
> And covered up our names.

Embodied in those lines is the major moral of the play, I think, because Tennessee, like E. M. Forster, believed that it was essential for human beings to "connect," to "communicate. "People need human contact," Shannon insists and the action of *The Night of the Iguana* centers on the breaking down of barriers between the characters, freeing them from their narrow cubicles and allowing them to reach out to each other.

In his poem about Herman Melville, W. H. Auden wrote that late in his life, the novelist "sailed into an extraordinary mildness,/ And anchored in his home . . . ," having learned that we are "introduced to Goodness every day" and his name is Billy Budd. Finally, for Melville, "The Godhead is broken like bread. We are the pieces." Tennessee seems to have undergone something of the same epiphany, and her name is Hannah Jelkes. With the setting free of the iguana, a "a little act of grace" on the part of Hannah and Shannon, and the setting free of Nonno, after the completion of his last poem, on God's part, and the consequent setting free of Hannah herself, peace has replaced the chaos in which the play began. Toward the end, Nonno says "it! is! finished!"—which are among the last words of Christ. Nonno's final poem, which is perhaps the best one Tennessee ever wrote, illuminates several themes of the play, including the Romantic dichotomy between the real ("the earth's obscene corrupting love") and the ideal worlds ("native green"), and the human need for grace and for courage in the face of one's always impending death.

Kenneth Holditch
New Orleans
June 2009

A SUMMER OF DISCOVERY

In those days there was, and for all I know still may be, a share-the-expense travel agency through which people whose funds were as limited as mine, that summer of 1940, got into contact with others who owned cars and were going in roughly the same direction.

A preliminary meeting and interview would be arranged in the office of the agency which was located in the lobby of a rather seedy midtown Manhattan hotel. It was about as embarrassing as applying for a job, perhaps even more so, for a man who is offering you a job can turn you down with some polite little dissimulation such as, "I'm looking for someone with a bit more experience in this type of work." But if you were turned down by a car-owner at this agency, you knew it could only be because you had failed to make an agreeable or trustworthy impression. Inevitably you were nervous and guilty-looking.

On this occasion, the summer that I had decided to go to Mexico for no more definite reason than that it was as far from New York as I could hope to get on the small funds at my disposal, the agency introduced me to a fantastic young honeymoon couple. The bridegroom was a young Mexican who had come up to New York to visit the World's Fair, then in progress, and had encountered and almost immediately married a young blonde lady of ambiguous profession whom he was now preparing to take home to meet his parents in Mexico City.

He had already met with so many unexpected expenses that he needed a paying passenger on his trip home, but it was obvious that my nervous manner aroused suspicion in him. Fortunately they had an interpreter with them, at the meeting, and the bride was more accustomed to and less distrustful of nervous young men. She felt nothing at all alarming about me, and through the interpreter persuaded her bridegroom to accept me as a traveling companion.

They didn't speak the same language in more ways than one and so the young lady, as the journey proceeded, began to use me as her confidant. About her ambiguous profession she had thoroughly deceived her new mate but she was very uncertain that his well-to-do parents in Mexico City, if we ever got there, would be equally gullible. And so, on the long way South, she would rap at my motel door almost every midnight to tell me about their latest misunderstanding or misadventure, and these clandestine conversations were the best psychological therapy that I could have had in my own state of anxiety and emotional turmoil, which was due to my feeling that my career as a Broadway playwright had stopped almost where it had started and what would follow was unpredictable but surely no good.

The journey was erratic as a blind bird's and took at least twice as long as would be reasonably expected, and the shared expenses were staggering by my standards. However my state of mind and emotion were so depressed that I was fairly indifferent to all practical concerns, even to a bad cold that turned to influenza, to the almost continual dream-state that comes with high fever and chills.

I never again saw this odd young couple after the morning when they delivered me to the YMCA building in Mexico City but, a year or two later, the bride sent me some fairly worthless articles of clothing which I had left in the trunk of the car, along with a note containing sentimental references to the wonderful trip that we had enjoyed together and hoping that sometime, somehow, we'd be able to enjoy another, and I thought to myself as I read it, this poor young woman has gone out of her mind.

Nobody had warned me that Mexico City was, in altitude, one of the highest cities in the world. I felt all the time as if I had taken Benzedrine, couldn't sleep, couldn't stay still. Surmising at last that I was allergic to atmosphere at the 7,500-foot level, I took a bus to Acapulco, some other young American having described it as a primitive place with much better swimming facilities than the "Y."

So I set out for Acapulco, with chills, fever, heart palpitations, and a mental state that was like a somnambulist's, apparently not bothering to inform Audrey Wood, my agent, the Theatre Guild, or the Dramatists Guild that my address would no longer be c/o General Delivery in Mexico City, an oversight which led to much complication some weeks later. Actually I was suffering from incipient tuberculosis, the scars of which are still visible on X-ray lung photos.

In Acapulco, I spent the first few days in a fantastic hotel near the central plaza. All the rooms opened onto a large patio-garden containing parrots, monkeys, and the proprietor of the hotel, who was so fat that he could hardly squeeze into a room at the place. Much of his time was devoted to cosmetic treatments which were administered in the patio. Every morning a very lively young barber would arrive to touch up the proprietor's hair with henna and give him a marcel wave and a cold cream facial. Since the dyed, waved hair was quite long and the proprietor spoke in a falsetto voice and was always clad in a bright silk kimono, I wasn't quite sure of his sex till I heard him addressed as Señor something-or-other by one of his employees.

The steaming hot squalor of that place quickly drove me to look for other accommodations, nearer the beaches. And that's how I discovered the background for my new play, *The Night of the Iguana*. I found a frame hotel called the Costa Verde on the hill over the still water beach called Caleta and stayed there from late August to late September.

It was a desperate period in my life, but it's during such times that we are most alive and they are the times that we remember most vividly, and a writer draws out of vivid and desperate intervals in his life the most necessary impulse or, drive toward his work, which is the transmutation of experience into some significant piece of creation, just as an oyster transforms, or covers over, the irritating grain of sand in his shell to a pearl, white or black, of lesser or greater value.

My daily program at the Costa Verde Hotel was the same as it had been everywhere else. I charged my nerves with strong black coffee, then went to my portable typewriter which was set on a card table on a verandah and worked till I was exhausted: then I ran down the hill to the still water beach for my swim.

One morning, taking my swim, I had a particularly bad fit of coughing. I tasted in my mouth something saltier than the waters of the Pacific and noticed beside my head, flowing from my mouth, a thin but bright thread of red blood. It was startling but not frightening to me, in fact I kept on swimming toward the opposite side of the bay, hardly bothering to look back to see if the trajectory of coughed-up blood was still trailing behind me, this being the summer when the prospect of death was hardly important to me.

What was important to me was the dreamworld of a new play. I have a theory that an artist will never die or go mad while he is engaged in a piece of work that is very important to him. All the cells of his body, all of his vital organs, as well as the brain cells in which volition is seated, seem to combine their forces to keep him alive and in control of his faculties. He may act crazily but he isn't crazy; he may show any symptom of mortality but he isn't dying.

As the world of reality in which I was caught began to dim out, as the work on the play continued, so did the death wish and the symptoms of it. And I remember this summer as the one when I got along best with people and when they seemed to like me, and I would attribute this condition to the fact that I expected to be dead before the summer was over and that there was consequently no reason for me to worry about what people thought of me. When you stop worrying what people think of you, you suddenly find yourself thinking of them, not yourself, and then, for the time that this condition remains, you have a sort of crazy charm for chance acquaintances such as the ones that were staying with me that crazy summer of 1940, at the Costa Verde in Acapulco.

By the middle of September the bleeding lungs had stopped bleeding, and the death wish had gone, and has never come back to me since. The only mementos of the summer are the scar on the X-ray plate, a story called "The Night of the Iguana," and now this play which has very little relation to the story except the same title and a bit of the same symbolism. But in both the short story and the play, written many years later, there is an incident of the capture of the iguana, which is a type of lizard, and its tying up under the verandah floor of the Costa Verde, which no longer exists in the new Acapulco.

Some critics resent my symbols, but let me ask, what would I do without them? Without my symbols I might still be employed by the International Shoe Co. in St. Louis.

Let me go further and say that unless the events of a life are translated into significant meanings, then life holds no more revelation than death, and possibly even less.

In September, that summer of 1940, the summer when, sick to death of myself, I turned to other people most truly, I discovered a human heart as troubled as my own. It was that of another young writer, a writer of magazine fiction who had just arrived from Tahiti because he feared that the war, which was then at a climax of fury, might cut him off from the magazines that purchased his adventure stories. But in Tahiti he had found that place which all of us spend our lives looking for, the one right home of the heart, and as the summer wore on I discovered that his desolation was greater than my own, since he was so despondent that he could no longer work.

There were hammocks along the sleeping verandahs. We would spend the evenings in adjacent hammocks, drinking rum-cocos, and discussing and comparing our respective heartbreaks, more and more peacefully as the night advanced.

It was an equinoctial season, and every night or so there would be a spectacular storm. I have never heard such thunder or seen such lightning except in melodramatic performances of Shakespeare. All of the inarticulate but passionate fury of the physical universe would sometimes be hurled at the hilltop and the verandah, and we were thrilled by it, it would completely eclipse our melancholy.

But the equinox wore itself out by late September, and we both returned to our gloomy introspections.

Day after steaming hot day I would go to Wells-Fargo in town for my option check and it wouldn't be there. It was long overdue and I was living on credit at the hotel, and I noticed, or suspected, a steady increase in the management's distrust of me.

I assumed that the Theatre Guild had dropped their option of *Battle of Angels* and lost all interest in me. The other young writer, still unable to scribble a line that he didn't scratch out with the groan of a dying beast, had no encouragement for me. He felt that it was quite clear that we had both arrived at the end of our ropes and that we'd better face it. We were both approaching the age of thirty, and he declared that we were not meant by implacable nature to go past that milestone, that it was the dead end for us.

Our gloom was not relieved by the presence of a party of German Nazis who were ecstatic over the early successes of the Luftwaffe over the R.A.F. When they were not gamboling euphorically on the beach, they were listening to the radio reports on the battle for Britain and their imminent conquest of it, and the entire demo-cratic world.

My writer friend began to deliver a pitch for suicide as the only decent and dignified way out for either of us. I disagreed with him, but very mildly.

Then one day the manager of the hotel told me that my credit had run out. I would have to leave the next morning, so that night my friend and I had more than our usual quota of rum-cocos, a drink that is prepared in a coconut shell by chopping off one end of it with a machete and mixing the juice of the nut with variable quantities of rum, a bit of lemon juice, a bit of sugar, and some cracked ice. You stick straws in the lopped-off end of the coconut and it's a long dreamy drink, the most delectable summer night's drink I've ever enjoyed, and that night we lay in our hammocks and had rum-cocos until the stars of the Southern Cross, which was visible in the sky from our veranda, began to flit crazily about like fireflies caught in a bottle.

My friend reverted to the subject of death as a preferable alter-native to life and was more than usually eloquent on the subject. It would have been logical for me to accept his argument but some-thing in me resisted. He said I was just being "chicken," that if I had any guts I would go down the hill with him, right then and now, and take "the long swim to China," as I was no more endur-ably situated on earth than he was.

All that I had, he told me, was the uncontrolled emotionalism of a minor lyric talent which was totally unsuited to the stage of life as well as the theater stage. I was, he said, a cotton-headed romanticist, a hopeless anachronism in the world now lit by super fire-bombs. He reeled out of his hammock and to the verandah steps, shouting, "Come on, you chicken, we're going to swim out to China!"

But I stayed in my hammock, and if he went swimming that night, it wasn't to China, for when I woke up in the hammock, and it was daylight, he was dressed and packed and had found an elderly tourist who had a car and was driving back to Texas, and had invited us to accompany him in his car free of charge. My friend hauled me out of the hammock and helped me pack for departure.

This old man, he declared, referring to our driver, is in the same boat as we are, and the best thing that could happen to all three of us is to miss a turn through the mountains and plunge off the road down a chasm, to everlasting oblivion. On this note, we cut out.

We had just reached the most hazardous section of the narrow road through the mountains when this other young writer asked the tourist if he couldn't take over the wheel for a while. Oh, no, I exclaimed. But the other writer insisted, and like a bat out of hell he took those hairpin turns through the Sierras. Any moment, I thought, we would surely crash into the mountain or plunge into the chasm on the road's other side, and it was then that I was all through with my death wish and knew that it was life that I longed for, on any terms that were offered.

I clenched my hands, bit my tongue, and kept praying. And gradually the driver's demonic spirit wore itself out, the car slowed, and he turned the wheel over to the owner and retired to the back seat to sleep off his aborted flirtation with the dark angel.

The Night of the Iguana is rooted in the atmosphere and experiences of the summer of 1940, which I remember more vividly, on the emotional level, than any summer that I have gone through before or after—since it was then, that summer, that I not only discovered that it was life that I truly longed for, but that all which is most valuable in life is escaping from the narrow cubicle of one's self to a sort of verandah between the sky and the still water beach (allegorically speaking) and to a hammock beside another beleaguered being, someone else who is in exile from the place and time of his heart's fulfillment.

A play that is more of a dramatic poem than a play is bound to rest on metaphorical ways of expression. Symbols and their meanings must be arrived at through a period of time which is often a long one, requiring much patience, but if you wait out this period of time, if you permit it to clear as naturally as a sky after a storm, it will reward you, finally, with a puzzle which is still puzzling but which, whether you fathom it or not, still has the beautifully disturbing sense of truth, as much of that ambiguous quality as we are permitted to know in all our seasons and travels and places of short stay on this risky planet.

At one point in the composition of this work it had an alternative title, *Two Acts of Grace,* a title which referred to a pair of desperate people who had the humble nobility of each putting the other's desperation, during the course of a night, above his concern for his own.

Being an unregenerate romanticist, even now, I can still think of nothing that gives more meaning to living.

Tennessee Williams

1961

THE NIGHT OF THE IGUANA
by Tennessee Williams

I

Opening onto the long South verandah of the Costa Verde hotel near Acapulco were ten sleeping rooms, each with a hammock slung outside its screen door. Only three of these rooms were occupied at the present time, for it was between the seasons at Acapulco. The winter season when the resort was more popular with the cosmopolitan type of foreign tourists had been over for a couple of months and the summer season when ordinary Mexican and American vacationists thronged there had not yet started. The three remaining guests of the Costa Verde were from the States, and they included two men who were writers and a Miss Edith Jelkes who had been an instructor in art at an Episcopalian girls' school in Mississippi until she had suffered a sort of nervous breakdown and had given up her teaching position for a life of refined vagrancy, made possible by an inherited income of about two hundred dollars a month.

Miss Jelkes was a spinster of thirty with a wistful blond prettiness and a somewhat archaic quality of refinement. She belonged to an historical Southern family of great but now moribund vitality whose latter generations had tended to split into two antithetical types, one in which the libido was pathologically distended and another in which it would seem to be all but dried up. The households were turbulently split and so, fairly often, were the personalities of their inmates. There had been an efflorescence among them of nervous talents and sickness, of drunkards and poets, gifted artists and sexual degenerates, together with fanatically proper and squeamish old ladies of both sexes who were condemned to live beneath the same roof with relatives whom they could only regard as monsters. Edith Jelkes was not strictly one or the other of the two basic types, which made it all the more difficult for her to cultivate any interior poise. She had been lucky enough to channel her somewhat morbid energy into a gift for painting. She painted canvases of an originality that might some day be noted, and in the meantime, since her retirement from teaching, she was combining her painting with travel and trying to evade her neurasthenia through the distraction of making new friends in new places. Perhaps some day she would come out on a kind of triumphant plateau as an artist or as a person or even perhaps as both. There might be a period of five or ten years in her life when she would serenely climb over the lightning-shot clouds of her immaturity and the waiting murk of decline. But perhaps is the right word to use. It would all depend on the next two years or so. For this reason she was particularly needful of sympathetic companionship, and the growing lack of it at the Costa Verde was really dangerous to her.

Miss Jelkes was outwardly such a dainty teapot that no one would guess that she could actually boil. She was so delicately made that rings and bracelets were never quite small enough originally to fit her but sections would have to be removed and the bands welded smaller. With her great translucent gray eyes and cloudy blond hair and perpetual look of slightly hurt confusion, she could not pass unnoticed through any group of strangers, and she knew how to dress in accord with her unearthly type. The cloudy blond hair was never without its flower and the throat of her cool white dresses would be set off by some vivid brooch of esoteric design. She loved the dramatic contrast of hot and cold color, the splash of scarlet on snow, which was like a flag of her own unsettled components. Whenever she came into a restaurant or theatre or exhibition gallery, she could hear or imagine that she could hear a little murmurous wave of appreciation. This was important to her, it had come to be one of her necessary comforts. But now that the guests of the Costa Verde had dwindled to herself and the two young writers—no matter how cool and yet vivid her appearance, there was little to comfort her in the way of murmured appreciation. The two young writers were bafflingly indifferent to Miss Jelkes. They barely turned their heads when she strolled onto the front or back verandah where they were lying in hammocks or seated at a table always carrying on a curiously intimate sounding conversation in tones never loud enough to be satisfactorily overheard by Miss Jelkes, and their responses to her friendly nods and Spanish phrases of greeting were barely distinct enough to pass for politeness.

Miss Jelkes was not at all inured to such offhand treatment. What had made travel so agreeable to her was the remarkable facility with which she had struck up acquaintances wherever she had gone. She was a good talker, she had a fresh and witty way of observing things. The many places she had been in the last six years had supplied her with a great reservoir of descriptive comment and humorous anecdote, and of course there was always the endless and epic chronicle of the Jelkeses to regale people with. Since she had just about the right amount of income to take her to the sort of hotels and *pensions* that are frequented by professional people such as painters and writers or professors on sabbatical leave, she had never before felt the lack of an appreciative audience. Things being as they were, she realized that the sensible action would be to simply withdraw to the Mexican capital where she had formed so many casual but nice connections among the American colony. Why she did not do this but remained on at the Costa Verde was not altogether clear to herself. Besides the lack of society there were other drawbacks to a continued stay. The food had begun to disagree with her, the Patrona of the hotel was becoming insolent and the service slovenly and her painting was showing signs of nervous distraction. There was every reason to leave, and yet she stayed on.

Miss Jelkes could not help knowing that she was actually conducting a siege of the two young writers, even though the reason for it was still entirely obscure.

She had set up her painting studio on the South verandah of the hotel where the writers worked in the mornings at their portable typewriters with their portable radio going off and on during pauses in their labor, but the comradeship of creation which she had hoped to establish was not forthcoming. Her eyes formed a habit of darting toward the two men as frequently as they did toward what she was painting, but her glances were not returned and her painting went into an irritating decline. She took to using her fingers more than her brushes, smearing and slapping on pigment with an impatient energy that defeated itself. Once in a while she would get up and wander as if absentmindedly down toward the writers' end of the long verandah, but when she did so, they would stop writing and stare blankly at their papers or into space until she had removed herself from their proximity, and once the younger writer had been so rude as to snatch his paper from the typewriter and turn it face down on the table as if he suspected her of trying to read it over his shoulder.

She had retaliated that evening by complaining to the Patrona that their portable radio was being played too loudly and too long, that it was keeping her awake at night, which she partially believed to be true, but the transmission of this complaint was not evidenced by any reduction in the volume or duration of the annoyance but by the writers' choice of a table at breakfast, the next morning, at the furthest possible distance from her own.

That day Miss Jelkes packed her luggage, thinking that she

would surely withdraw the next morning, but her curiosity about the two writers, especially the older of the two, had now become so obsessive that not only her good sense but her strong natural dignity was being discarded.

Directly below the cliff on which the Costa Verde was planted there was a small private beach for the hotel guests. Because of her extremely fair skin it had been Miss Jelkes' practice to bathe only in the early morning or late afternoon when the glare was diminished. These hours did not coincide with those of the writers who usually swam and sunbathed between two and six in the afternoon. Miss Jelkes now began to go down to the beach much earlier without admitting to herself that it was for the purpose of espionage. She would now go down to the beach about four o'clock in the afternoon and she would situate herself as close to the two young men as she could manage without being downright brazen. Bits of their background and history had begun to filter through this unsatisfactory contact. It became apparent that the younger of the men, who was about twenty-five, had been married and recently separated from a wife he called Kitty. More from the inflection of voices than the fragmentary sentences that she caught, Miss Jelkes received the impression that he was terribly concerned over some problem which the older man was trying to iron out for him. The younger one's voice would sometimes rise in agitation loudly enough to be overheard quite plainly. He would cry out phrases such as *For God's sake* or *What the Hell are you talking about!* Sometimes his language was so strong that Miss Jelkes winced with embarrassment and he would sometimes pound the wet sand with his palm and hammer it with his heels like a child in a tantrum. The older man's voice would also be lifted briefly. Don't be a fool, he would shout. Then his voice would drop to a low and placating tone. The conversation would fall below the level of audibility once more. It seemed that some argument was going on almost interminably between them. Once Miss Jelkes was astonished to see the younger one jump to his feet with an in-coherent outcry and start kicking sand directly into the face of his older companion. He did it quite violently and hatefully, but the older man only laughed and grabbed the younger one's feet and restrained them until the youth dropped back beside him, and then they had surprised Miss Jelkes even further by locking their hands together and lying in silence until the incoming tide was lapping over their bodies. Then they had both jumped up, apparently in good humor, and made racing dives in the water.

Because of this troubled youth and wise counsellor air of their conversations it had at first struck Miss Jelkes, in the beginning of her preoccupation with them, that the younger man might be a war veteran suffering from shock and that the older one might be a doctor who had brought him down to the Pacific resort while conducting a psychiatric treatment. This was before she discov-ered the name of the older man, on mail addressed to him. She had instantly recognized the name as one that she had seen time and again on the covers of literary magazines and as the author of a novel that had caused a good deal of controversy a few years ago. It was a novel that dealt with some sensational subject. She had not read it and could not remember what the subject was but the name was associated in her mind with a strongly social kind of writing which had been more in vogue about five years past than it was since the beginning of the war. However the writer was still not more than thirty. He was not good-looking but his face had distinction. There was something a little monkey-like in his face as there frequently is in the faces of serious young writ-ers, a look that reminded Miss Jelkes of a small chimpanzee she had once seen in the corner of his cage at a zoo, just sitting there staring between the bars, while all his fellows were hopping and spinning about on their noisy iron trapeze. She remembered how she had been touched by his solitary position and lackluster eyes. She had wanted to give him some peanuts but the elephants had devoured all she had. She had returned to the vendor to buy some more but when she brought them to the chimpanzee's cage, he had evidently succumbed to the general impulse, for now every man Jack of them was hopping and spinning about on the clanking trapeze and not a one of them seemed a bit different from the others. Looking at this writer she felt almost an identical urge to share something with him, but the wish was thwarted again, in this instance by a studious will to ignore her. It was not accidental, the way that he kept his eyes off her. It was the same on the beach as it was on the hotel verandahs.

On the beach he wore next to nothing, a sort of brilliant diaper of printed cotton, twisted about his loins in a fashion that sometimes failed to even approximate decency, but he had a slight and graceful physique and an unconscious ease of movement which made the immodesty less offensive to Miss Jelkes than it was in the case of his friend. The younger man had been an athlete at college and he was massively constructed. His torso was burned the color of an old penny and its emphatic gender still further exclaimed by luxuriant patterns of hair, sunbleached till it shone like masses of crisped and frizzed golden wire. Moreover his regard for propriety was so slight that he would get in and out of his colorful napkin as if he were standing in a private cabana. Miss Jelkes had to acknowledge that he owned a certain sculptural grandeur but the spinsterish side of her nature was still too strong to permit her to feel anything but a squeamish distaste. This reaction of Miss Jelkes was so strong on one occasion that when she had returned to the hotel she went directly to the Patrona to enquire if the younger gentleman could not be persuaded to change clothes in his room or, if this was too much to ask of him, that he might at least keep the dorsal side of his nudity toward the beach. The Patrona was very much interested in the complaint but not in a way that Miss Jelkes had hoped she would be. She laughed immoderately, translating phrases of Miss Jelkes' complaint into idiomatic Spanish, shouted to the waiters and the cook. All of them joined in the laughter and the noise was still going on when Miss Jelkes standing confused and indignant saw the two young men climbing up the hill. She retired quickly to her room on the hammock-verandah but she knew by the reverberating merriment on the other side that the writers were being told, and that all of the Costa Verde was holding her up to undisguised ridicule. She started packing at once, this time not even bothering to fold things neatly into her steamer trunk, and she was badly frightened, so much disturbed that it affected her stomach and the following day she was not well enough to undertake a journey.

It was this following day that the Iguana was caught.

The Iguana is a lizard, two or three feet in length, which the Mexicans regard as suitable for the table. They are not always eaten right after they are caught but being creatures that can survive for quite a while without food or drink, they are often held in captivity for some time before execution. Miss Jelkes had been told that they tasted rather like chicken, which opinion she ascribed to a typically Mexican way of glossing over an unappetizing fact. What bothered her about the Iguana was the inhumanity of its treatment during its interval of captivity. She had seen them outside the huts of villagers, usually hitched to a short pole near the doorway and continually and hopelessly clawing at the dry earth within the orbit of the rope-length, while naked children squatted around it, poking it with sticks in the eyes and mouth.

Now the Patrona's adolescent son had captured one of these Iguanas and had fastened it to the base of a column under the hammock-verandah. Miss Jelkes was not aware of its presence until late the night of the capture. Then she had been disturbed by the scuffling sound it made and had slipped on her dressing gown and had gone out in the bright moonlight to discover what the sound was caused by. She looked over the rail of the verandah and she saw the Iguana hitched to the base of the column nearest her doorway and making the most pitiful effort to scramble into the bushes just beyond the taut length of its rope. She uttered a little cry of horror as she made this discovery.

The two young writers were lying in hammocks at the other end of the verandah and as usual were carrying on a desultory conversation in tones not loud enough to carry to her bedroom.

Without stopping to think, and with a curious thrill of exultation, Miss Jelkes rushed down to their end of the verandah. As she drew near them she discovered that the two writers were engaged in drinking rum-coco, which is a drink prepared in the shell of a coconut by knocking a cap off it with a machete and pouring into the nut a mixture of rum, lemon, sugar and cracked ice. The drinking had been going on since supper and the floor beneath their two hammocks was littered with bits of white pulp and hairy brown fibre and was so slippery that Miss Jelkes barely kept her footing. The liquid had spilt over their faces, bare throats and chests, giving them an oily lustre, and about their hammocks was hanging a cloud of moist and heavy sweetness. Each had a leg thrown over the edge of the hammock with which he pushed himself lazily back and forth. If Miss Jelkes had been seeing them for the first time, the gross details of the spectacle would have been more than association with a few dissolute members of the Jelkes family had prepared her to stomach, and she would have scrupulously avoided a second glance at them. But Miss Jelkes had been changing more than she was aware of during this period of preoccupation with the two writers, her scruples were more undermined than she suspected, so that if the word *pigs* flashed through her mind for a moment, it failed to distract her even momentarily from what she was bent on doing. It was a form of hysteria that had taken hold of her, her action and her speech were without volition.

"Do you know what has happened!" she gasped as she came toward them. She came nearer than she would have consciously dared, so that she was standing directly over the young writer's prone figure. "That horrible boy, the son of the Patrona, has tied up an Iguana beneath my bedroom. I heard him tying it up but I didn't know what it was. I've been listening to it for hours, ever since supper, and didn't know what it was. Just now I got up to investigate, I looked over the edge of the verandah and there it was, scuffling around at the end of its little rope!"

Neither of the writers said anything for a moment, but the older one had propped himself up a little to stare at Miss Jelkes.

"There *what* was?" he enquired.

"She is talked about the Iguana," said the younger.

"Oh! Well, what about it?"

"How can I sleep?" cried Miss Jelkes. "How could anyone sleep with that example of Indian savagery right underneath my door!"

"You have an aversion to lizards?" suggested the older writer.

"I have an aversion to brutality!" corrected Miss Jelkes.

"But the lizard is a very low grade of animal life. Isn't it a very low grade of animal life?" he asked his companion.

"Not as low as some," said the younger writer. He was grinning maliciously at Miss Jelkes, but she did not notice him at all, her attention was fixed upon the older writer.

"At any rate," said the writer, "I don't believe it is capable of feeling half as badly over its misfortune as you seem to be feeling for it."

"I don't agree with you," said Miss Jelkes. "I don't agree with you at all! We like to think that we are the only ones that are capable of suffering but that is just human conceit. We are not the only ones that are capable of suffering. Why, even plants have sensory impressions. I have seen some that closed their leaves when you touched them!"

She held out her hand and drew her slender fingers into a chalice that closed. As she did this she drew a deep, tortured breath with her lips pursed and nostrils flaring and her eyes rolled heavenwards so that she looked like a female Saint on the rack.

The younger man chuckled but the older one continued to stare at her gravely.

"I am sure," she went on, "that the Iguana has very definite feelings, and you would be, too, if you had been listening to it, scuffling around out there in that awful dry dust, trying to reach the bushes with that rope twisted about its neck, making it almost impossible for it to breathe!"

She clutched her throat as she spoke and with the other hand made a clawing gesture in the air. The younger writer broke into a laugh, the older one smiled at Miss Jelkes.

"You have a real gift," he said, "for vicarious experience."

"Well, I just can't stand to witness suffering," said Miss Jelkes. "I can endure it myself but I just can't stand to witness it in others, no matter whether it's human suffering or animal suffering. And there is so much suffering in the world, so much that is necessary suffering, such as illnesses and accidents which cannot be avoided. But there is so much unnecessary suffering, too, so much that is inflicted simply because some people have a callous disregard for the feelings of others. Sometimes it almost seems as if the universe was designed by the Marquis de Sade!"

She threw back her head with an hysterical laugh.

"And I do not believe in the principle of atonement," she went on. "Isn't it awful, isn't it really preposterous that practically all our religions should be based on the principle of atonement when there is really and truly no such thing as guilt?"

"I am sorry," said the older writer. He rubbed his forehead. "I am not in any condition to talk about God."

"Oh, I'm not talking about God," said Miss Jelkes. "I'm talking about the Iguana!"

"She's trying to say that the Iguana is one of God's creatures," said the younger writer.

"But that one of God's creatures," said the older, "is now in the possession of the Patrona's son!"

"That one of God's creatures," Miss Jelkes exclaimed, "is now hitched to a post right underneath my door, and late as it is I have a very good notion to go and wake up the Patrona and tell her that they have got to turn it loose or at least to remove it some place where I can't hear it!"

The younger writer was now laughing with drunken vehemence. "What are you bellowing over?" the older one asked him.

"If she goes and wakes up the Patrona, anything can happen!"

"What?" asked Miss Jelkes. She glanced uncertainly at both of them.

"That's quite true," said the older. "One thing these Mexicans will not tolerate is the interruption of sleep!"

"But what can she do but apologize and remove it!" demanded Miss Jelkes. "Because after all, it's a pretty outrageous thing to hitch a lizard beneath a woman's door and expect her to sleep with that noise going on all night!"

"It might not go on all night," said the older writer.

"What's going to stop it?" asked Miss Jelkes.

"The Iguana might go to sleep."

"Never!" said Miss Jelkes. "The creature is frantic and what it is going through must be a nightmare!"

"You're bothered a good deal by noises?" asked the older writer. This was, of course, a dig at Miss Jelkes for her complaint about the radio. She recognized it as such and welcomed the chance it gave to defend and explain. In fact this struck her as being the golden moment for breaking all barriers down.

"That's true, I am!" she admitted breathlessly. "You see, I had a nervous breakdown a few years ago, and while I'm ever so much better than I was, sleep is more necessary to me than it is to people who haven't gone through a terrible thing like that. Why, for months and months I wasn't able to sleep without a sedative tablet, sometimes two of them a night! Now I hate like anything to be a nuisance to people, to make unreasonable demands, because

I am always so anxious to get along well with people, not only peaceably, but really *cordially* with them—even with strangers that I barely *speak* to—However it sometimes happens . . ."

She paused for a moment. A wonderful thought had struck her.

"I know what I'll do!" she cried out. She gave the older writer a radiant smile.

"What's that?" asked the younger. His tone was full of suspicion but Miss Jelkes smiled at him, too.

"Why, I'll just move!" she said.

"Out of Costa Verde?" suggested the younger.

"Oh, no, no, no! No, indeed! It's the nicest resort hotel I've ever stopped at! I mean that I'll change my room."

"Where will you change it to?"

"Down here," said Miss Jelkes, "to this end of the verandah! I won't even wait till morning. I'll move right now. All these vacant rooms, there couldn't be any objection, and if there is, why, I'll just explain how totally impossible it was for me to sleep with that lizard's commotion all night!"

She turned quickly about on her heels, so quickly that she nearly toppled over on the slippery floor, caught her breath laughingly and rushed back to her bedroom. Blindly she swept up a few of her belongings in her arms and rushed back to the writers' end of the verandah where they were holding a whispered consultation.

"Which is your room?" she asked.

"We have two rooms," said the younger writer coldly.

"Yes, one each," said the older.

"Oh, of course!" said Miss Jelkes. "But I don't want to make the embarrassing error of confiscating one of you gentlemen's beds!"

She laughed gaily at this. It was the sort of remark she would make to show new acquaintances how far from being formal and prudish she was. But the writers were not inclined to laugh with her, so she cleared her throat and started blindly toward the nearest door, dropping a comb and a mirror as she did so.

"Seven years bad luck!" said the younger man.

"It isn't broken!" she gasped.

"Will you help me?" she asked the older writer.

He got up unsteadily and put the dropped articles back on the disorderly pile in her arms.

"I'm sorry to be so much trouble!" she gasped pathetically. Then she turned again to the nearest doorway.

"Is this one vacant?"

"No, that's mine," said the younger.

"Then how about *this* one?"

"That one is mine," said the older.

"Sounds like the Three Bears and Goldilocks!" laughed Miss Jelkes. "Well, oh, dear—I guess I'll just have to take *this* one!"

She rushed to the screen door on the other side of the younger writer's room, excitingly aware as she did so that this would put her within close range of their nightly conversations, the mystery of which had tantalized her for weeks. Now she would be able to hear every word that passed between them unless they actually whispered in each other's ear!

She rushed into the bedroom and let the screen door slam.

She switched on the suspended light bulb and hastily plunged the articles borne with her about a room that was identical with the one that she had left and then plopped herself down upon an identical white iron bed.

There was silence on the verandah.

Without rising she reached above her to pull the cord of the light bulb. Its watery yellow glow was replaced by the crisp white flood of moonlight through the gauze-netted window and through the screen of the door.

She lay flat on her back with her arms lying rigidly along her sides and every nerve tingling with excitement over the spontaneous execution of a piece of strategy carried out more expertly than it would have been after days of preparation.

For a while the silence outside her new room continued.

Then the voice of the younger writer pronounced the word "Goldilocks!"

Two shouts of laughter rose from the verandah. It continued without restraint till Miss Jelkes could feel her ears burning in the dark as if rays of intense light were concentrated on them.

There was no more talk that evening, but she heard their feet scraping as they got off the hammocks and walked across the verandah to the further steps and down them.

Miss Jelkes was badly hurt, worse than she had been hurt the previous afternoon, when she had complained about the young man's immodesty on the beach. As she lay there upon the severe white bed that smelled of ammonia, she could feel coming toward her one of those annihilating spells of neurasthenia which had led to her breakdown six years ago. She was too weak to cope with it, it would have its way with her and bring her God knows how close to the verge of lunacy and even possibly over! What an intolerable burden, and why did she have to bear it, she who was so humane and gentle by nature that even the sufferings of a lizard could hurt her! She turned her face to the cold white pillow and wept. She wished that she were a writer. If she were a writer it would be possible to say things that only Picasso had ever put into paint. But if she said them, would anybody believe them? Was her sense of the enormous grotesquerie of the world communicable to any other person? And why should it be told if it could be? And why, most of all, did she make such a fool of herself in her frantic need to find some comfort in people!

She felt that the morning was going to be pitilessly hot and bright and she turned over in her mind the list of neuroses that might fasten upon her. Everything that is thoughtless and automatic in healthy organisms might take on for her an air of preposterous novelty. The act of breathing and the beat of her heart and the very process of thinking would be self-conscious if this worst-of-all neuroses should take hold of her—and take hold of her it would, because she was so afraid of it! The precarious balance of her nerves would be all overthrown. Her entire being would turn into a feverish little machine for the production of fears, fears that could not be put into words because of their all-encompassing immensity, and even supposing that they could be put into language and so be susceptible to the comfort of telling—who was there at the Costa Verde, this shadowless rock by the ocean, that she could turn to except the two young writers who seemed to despise her? How awful to be at the mercy of merciless people!

Now I'm indulging in self-pity, she thought.

She turned on her side and fished among articles on the bed table for the little cardboard box of sedative tablets. They would get her through the night, but tomorrow—oh, tomorrow! She lay there senselessly trying, hearing even at this distance the efforts of the captive Iguana to break from its rope and scramble into the bushes . . .

II

When Miss Jelkes awoke it was still a while before morning. The moon, however, had disappeared from the sky and she was lying in blackness that would have been total except for tiny cracks of light that came through the wall of the adjoining bedroom, the one that was occupied by the younger writer.

It did not take her long to discover that the younger writer was not alone in his room. There was no speech but the quality of sounds that came at intervals though the partition made her certain the room had two people in it.

If she could have risen from bed and peered through one of the cracks without betraying herself she might have done so, but knowing that any move would be overheard, she remained on the bed and her mind was now alert with suspicions which had before been only a formless wonder.

At last she heard someone speak.

"You'd better turn out the light," said the voice of the younger writer.

"Why?"

"There are cracks in the wall."

"So much the better. I'm sure that's why she moved down here."

The younger one raised his voice.

"You don't think she moved because of the Iguana?"

"Hell, no, that was just an excuse. Didn't you notice how pleased she was with herself, as if she had pulled off something downright brilliant?"

"I bet she's eavesdropping on us right this minute," said the younger.

"Undoubtedly she is. But what can she do about it?"

"Go to the Patrona."

Both of them laughed.

"The Patrona wants to get rid of her," said the younger.

"Does she?"

"Yep. She's crazy to have her move out. She's even given the cook instructions to put too much salt in her food."

They both laughed.

Miss Jelkes discovered that she had risen from the bed. She was standing uncertainly on the cold floor for a moment and then she was rushing out of the screen door and up to the door of the younger writer's bedroom.

She knocked on the door, carefully keeping her eyes away from the lighted interior.

"Come in," said a voice.

"I'd rather not," said Miss Jelkes. "Will you come here for a minute?"

"Sure," said the younger writer. He stepped to the door, wearing only the trousers to his pyjamas.

"Oh," he said. "It's you!"

She stared at him without any idea of what she had come to say or had hoped to accomplish.

"Well?" he demanded brutally.

"I—I heard you!" she stammered.

"So?"

"I don't understand it!"

"What?"

"Cruelty! I never could understand it!"

"But you do understand spying, don't you?"

"I wasn't spying!" she cried.

He muttered a shocking word and shoved past her onto the porch.

The older writer called his name: "Mike!" But he only repeated the shocking word more loudly and walked away from them. Miss Jelkes and the older writer faced each other. The violence just past had calmed Miss Jelkes a little. She found herself uncoiling inside and comforting tears beginning to moisten her eyes. Outside the night was changing. A wind had sprung up and the surf that broke on the other side of the landlocked bay called Coleta could now be heard.

"It's going to storm," said the writer.

"Is it? I'm glad!" said Miss Jelkes.

"Won't you come in?"

"I'm not at all properly dressed."

"I'm not either."

"Oh, well—"

She came in. Under the naked light bulb and without the dark glasses his face looked older and the eyes, which she had not seen before, had a look that often goes with incurable illness.

She noticed that he was looking about for something.

"Tablets," he muttered.

She caught sight of them first, among a litter of papers. She handed them to him.

"Thank you. Will you have one?"

"I've had one already."

"What kind are yours?"

"Seconal. Yours?"

"Barbital. Are yours good?"

"Wonderful."

"How do they make you feel? Like a water-lily?"

"Yes, like a water lily on a Chinese lagoon!"

Miss Jelkes laughed with real gaiety but the writer responded only with a faint smile. His attention was drifting away from her again. He stood at the screen door like a worried child awaiting the return of a parent.

"Perhaps I should—"

Her voice faltered. She did not want to leave. She wanted to stay there. She felt herself upon the verge of saying incommunicable things to this man whose singularity was so like her own in many essential respects, but his turned back did not invite her to stay. He shouted the name of his friend. There was no response. The writer turned back from the door with a worried muttering but his attention did not return to Miss Jelkes.

"Your friend—" she faltered.

"Mike?"

"Is he the—right person for you?"

"Mike is helpless and I am always attracted by helpless people."

"But you," she said awkwardly. "How about you? Don't you need somebody's help?"

"The help of God!" said the writer. "Failing that, I have to depend on myself."

"But isn't it possible that with somebody else, somebody with more understanding, more like *yourself*—!"

"You mean *you?*" he asked bluntly.

Miss Jelkes was spared the necessity of answering one way or another, for at that moment a great violence was unleashed outside the screen door. The storm that had hovered uncertainly on the horizon was now plunging toward them. Not continually but in sudden thrusts and withdrawals, like a giant bird lunging up and down on its terrestrial quarry, a bird with immense white wings and beak of godlike fury, the attack was delivered against the jut of rock on which the Costa Verde was planted. Time and again the whole night blanched and trembled, but there was something frustrate in the attack of the storm. It seemed to be one that came from a thwarted will. Otherwise surely the frame structure would have been smashed. But the giant white bird did not know where it was striking. Its beak of fury was blind, or perhaps the beak—

It may have been that Miss Jelkes was right on the verge of divining more about God than a mortal ought to—when suddenly the writer leaned forward and thrust his knees between hers. She noticed that he had removed the towel about him and now was quite naked. She did not have time to wonder nor even to feel much surprise for in the next few moments, and for the first time in her thirty years of preordained spinsterhood, she was enacting a fierce little comedy of defense. He thrust at her like the bird of blind white fury. His one hand attempted to draw up the skirt of her robe while his other tore at the flimsy goods at her bosom. The upper cloth tore. She cried out with pain as the predatory fingers dug into her flesh. But she did not give in. Not she herself resisted but some demon of virginity that occupied her flesh fought off the assailant more furiously than he attacked her. And her demon won, for all at once the man let go of her gown and his fingers released her bruised bosom. A sobbing sound in his throat, he collapsed against her. She felt a wing-like throbbing against her belly, and then a scalding wetness. Then he let go of her altogether. She

178

sank back into her chair which had remained demurely upright throughout the struggle, as unsuitably, as ridiculously, as she herself had maintained her upright position. The man was sobbing. And then the screen door opened and the younger writer came in. Automatically Miss Jelkes freed herself from the damp embrace of her unsuccessful assailant.

"What is it?" asked the younger writer.

He repeated his question several times, senselessly but angrily, while he shook his older friend who could not stop crying.

I don't belong here, thought Miss Jelkes, and suiting action to thought, she slipped quietly out the screen door. She did not turn back into the room immediately adjoining but ran down the verandah to the room she had occupied before. She threw herself onto the bed which was now as cool as if she had never lain on it. She was grateful for that and for the abrupt cessation of fury outside. The white bird had gone away and the Costa Verde had survived its assault. There was nothing but the rain now, pattering without much energy, and the far away sound of the ocean only a little more distinct than it had been before the giant bird struck. She remembered the Iguana.

Oh, yes, the Iguana! She lay there with ears pricked for the painful sound of its scuffling, but there was no sound but the effortless flowing of water. Miss Jelkes could not contain her curiosity so at last she got out of bed and looked over the edge of the verandah. She saw the rope. She saw the whole length of the rope lying there in a relaxed coil, but not the Iguana. Somehow or other the creature tied by the rope had gotten away. Was it an act of God that effected this deliverance? Or was it not more reasonable to suppose that only Mike, the beautiful and helpless and cruel, had cut the Iguana loose? No matter. No matter who did it, the Iguana was gone, had scrambled back into its native bushes and, oh, how gratefully it must be breathing now! And she was grateful, too, for in some equally mysterious way the strangling rope of her loneliness had also been severed by what had happened tonight on this barren rock above the moaning waters.

Now she was sleepy. But just before falling asleep she remembered and felt again the spot of dampness, now turning cool but still adhering to the flesh of her belly as a light but persistent kiss. Her fingers approached it timidly. They expected to draw back with revulsion but were not so affected. They touched it curiously and even pityingly and did not draw back for a while. *Ah, Life,* she thought to herself and was about to smile at the originality of this thought when darkness lapped over the outward gaze of her mind.

1948

A CHRONOLOGY

1907   June 3: Cornelius Coffin Williams and Edwina Estelle Dakin marry in Columbus, Mississippi.

1909   November 19: Sister, Rose Isabelle Williams, is born in Columbus, Mississippi.

1911   March 26: Thomas Lanier Williams III is born in Columbus, Mississippi.

1918   July: Williams family moves to St. Louis, Missouri.

1919   February 21: Brother, Walter Dakin Williams, is born in St. Louis, Missouri.

1928   Short story "The Vengeance of Nitocris" is published in *Weird Tales* magazine.

        July: Williams's grandfather, Walter Edwin Dakin (1857–1954), takes young Tom on a tour of Europe.

1929   September: Begins classes at the University of Missouri at Columbia.

1930   Writes the one-act play *Beauty is the Word* for a local contest.

1932   Summer: Fails ROTC and is taken out of college by his father and put to work as a clerk at the International Shoe Company.

1936   January: Enrolls in extension courses at Washington University, St. Louis.

1937   March 18 and 20: First full-length play, *Candles to the Sun*, is produced by the Mummers, a semi-professional theater company in St. Louis.

September: Transfers to the University of Iowa.

November 30 and December 4: *Fugitive Kind* is performed by the Mummers.

1938   Graduates from the University of Iowa with a degree in English.

Completes the play *Not About Nightingales*.

1939   *Story* magazine publishes "The Field of Blue Children" with the first printed use of his professional name, "Tennessee Williams."

Receives an award from the Group Theatre for a group of short plays collectively titled *American Blues*, which leads to his association with Audrey Wood, his agent for the next thirty-two years.

1940   January through June: Studies playwriting with John Gassner at the New School for Social Research in New York City.

December 30: *Battle of Angels*, starring Miriam Hopkins, suffers a disastrous first night during its out-of-town try-out in Boston and closes shortly thereafter.

1942   December: At a cocktail party thrown by Lincoln Kirstein in New York, meets James Laughlin, founder of New Directions, who is to become Williams' lifelong friend and publisher.

1943   January 13: A bilateral prefrontal lobotomy is performed on Rose Isabelle Williams, leaving her in a childlike mental state for the rest of her life.

Drafts a screenplay, *The Gentleman Caller*, while under contract in Hollywood with Metro Goldwyn Mayer: rejected by the studio, he later rewrites it as *The Glass Menagerie*.

October 13: A collaboration with his friend Donald Windham, *You Touched Me!* (based on a story by D. H. Lawrence), premieres at the Cleveland Playhouse.

1944   December 26: *The Glass Menagerie* opens in Chicago starring Laurette Taylor.

A group of poems titled "The Summer Belvedere" is published in *Five Young American Poets, 1944*. (All books listed here are published by New Directions unless otherwise indicated.)

1945   March 25: *Stairs to the Roof* premieres at the Pasadena Playhouse in California.

March 31: *The Glass Menagerie* opens on Broadway and goes on to win the Drama Critics Circle Award for best play of the year.

September 25: *You Touched Me!* opens on Broadway, and is later published by Samuel French.

December 27: *Wagons Full of Cotton and Other Plays* is published.

1947   Summer: Meets Frank Merlo (1929–1963) in Provincetown—starting in 1948 they become lovers and companions, and remain together for fourteen years.

December 3: *A Streetcar Named Desire,* directed by Elia Kazan and starring Jessica Tandy, Marlon Brando, Kim Hunter and Karl Malden, opens on Broadway to rave reviews and wins the Pulitzer Prize and the Drama Critics Circle Award.

1948   October 6: *Summer and Smoke* opens on Broadway and closes in just over three months.

1949   January: *One Arm and Other Stories* is published.

1950   The novel *The Roman Spring of Mrs. Stone* is published.

The film version of *The Glass Menagerie* is released.

1951   February 3: *The Rose Tattoo* opens on Broadway starring Maureen Stapleton and Eli Wallach and wins the Tony Award for best play of the year.

The film version of *A Streetcar Named Desire* is released starring Vivian Leigh as Blanche and Marlon Brando as Stanley.

1952   April 24: A revival of *Summer and Smoke* directed by José Quintero and starring Geraldine Page opens off-Broadway at the Circle at the Square and is a critical success.

The National Institute of Arts and Letters inducts Williams as a member.

1953   March 19: *Camino Real* opens on Broadway and after a harsh critical reception closes within two months.

1954   A book of stories, *Hard Candy*, is published in August.

1955   March 24: *Cat on a Hot Tin Roof* opens on Broadway directed by Elia Kazan and starring Barbara Bel Geddes, Ben Gazzara and Burl Ives. *Cat* wins the Pulitzer Prize and the Drama Critics Circle Award.

The film version of *The Rose Tattoo*, for which Anna Magnani later wins an Academy Award, is released.

1956   The film *Baby Doll*, with a screenplay by Williams and directed by Elia Kazan, is released amid some controversy and is blacklisted by Catholic leader Cardinal Spellman.

June: *In the Winter of Cities*, Williams's first book of poetry, is published.

1957   March 21: *Orpheus Descending*, a revised version of *Battle of Angels*, directed by Harold Clurman, opens on Broadway but closes after two months.

1958   February 7: *Suddenly Last Summer* and *Something Unspoken* open off-Broadway under the collective title *Garden District*.

        The film version of *Cat on a Hot Tin Roof* is released.

1959   March 10: *Sweet Bird of Youth* opens on Broadway and runs for three months.

        The film version of *Suddenly Last Summer*, with a screenplay by Gore Vidal, is released.

1960   November 10: The comedy *Period of Adjustment* opens on Broadway and runs for over four months.

        The film version of *Orpheus Descending* is released under the title *The Fugitive Kind*.

1961   December 29: *The Night of the Iguana* opens on Broadway and runs for nearly ten months.

        The film versions of *Summer and Smoke* and *The Roman Spring of Mrs. Stone* are released.

1962   The film versions of *Sweet Bird of Youth* and *Period of Adjustment* are released.

1963   January 15: *The Milk Train Doesn't Stop Here Anymore* opens on Broadway and closes immediately due to a blizzard and a newspaper strike. It is revived January 1, 1964, in a Broadway production starring Tallulah Bankhead and Tab Hunter and closes within a week.

        September: Frank Merlo dies of lung cancer.

1964   The film version of *Night of the Iguana* is released.

1966   February 22: *Slapstick Tragedy* (*The Mutilated* and *The Gnädiges Fräulein*) runs on Broadway for less than a week.

        December: A novella and stories are published under the title *The Knightly Quest*.

1968   March 27: *Kingdom of Earth* opens on Broadway under the title *The Seven Descents of Myrtle*.

The film version of *The Milk Train Doesn't Stop Here Anymore* is released under the title *Boom!*

1969   May 11: *In the Bar of a Tokyo Hotel* opens off-Broadway and runs for three weeks.

Committed by his brother Dakin for three months to the Renard Psychiatric Division of Barnes Hospital in St. Louis.

The film version of *Kingdom of Earth* is released under the title *The Last of the Mobile Hot Shots*.

Awarded Doctor of Humanities degree by the University of Missouri and a Gold Medal for Drama by the American Academy of Arts and Letters.

1970   February: A book of plays, *Dragon Country*, is published.

1971   Williams breaks with his agent Audrey Wood. Bill Barnes assumes his representation, and then later Mitch Douglas.

1972   April 2: *Small Craft Warnings* opens off-Broadway.

Williams is given a Doctor of Humanities degree by the University of Hartford.

1973   March 1: *Out Cry*, the revised version of *The Two-Character Play*, opens on Broadway.

1974   September: *Eight Mortal Ladies Possessed*, a book of short stories, is published.

Williams is presented with an Entertainment Hall of Fame Award and a Medal of Honor for Literature from the National Arts Club.

1975   The novel *Moise and the World of Reason* is published by Simon and Schuster and Williams's *Memoirs* is published by Doubleday.

1976   January 20: *This Is* (*An Entertainment*) opens in San Francisco at the American Conservatory Theater.

June: *The Red Devil Battery Sign* closes during its out-of-town tryout in Boston.

November 23: *Eccentricities of a Nightingale*, a rewritten version of *Summer and Smoke*, opens in New York.

April: Williams's second volume of poetry, *Androgyne, Mon Amour*, is published.

1977   May 11: *Vieux Carré* opens on Broadway and closes within two weeks.

1978   *Tiger Tail* premieres at the Alliance Theater in Atlanta, Georgia, and a revised version premieres the following year at the Hippodrome Theater in Gainsville, Florida.

1979   January 10: *A Lovely Sunday for Creve Coeur* opens off-Broadway.

Kirche, Küche, Kinder workshops off-Broadway at the Jean Cocteau Repertory Theater.

Williams is presented with a Lifetime Achievement Award at the Kennedy Center Honors in Washington by President Jimmy Carter.

1980   January 25: *Will Mr. Merriwether Return from Memphis?* premieres for a limited run at the Tennessee Williams Performing Arts Center in Key West, Florida.

March 26: Williams's last Broadway play, *Clothes for a Summer Hotel*, opens and closes after 15 performances.

1981   August 24: *Something Cloudy, Something Clear* premieres off-Broadway at the Jean Cocteau Repertory Theater.

1982   May 8: The second of two versions of *A House Not Meant to Stand* opens for a limited run at the Goodman Theater in Chicago.

1983   February 24: Williams is found dead in his room at the Hotel Elysee in New York City. It is determined from an autopsy that the playwright died from asphyxiation, choking on a plastic medicine cap. Williams is later buried in St. Louis.

1984   July: *Stopped Rocking and Other Screenplays* is published.

1985   November: *Collected Stories*, with an introduction by Gore Vidal, is published.

1995   The first half of Lyle Leverich's important biography, *Tom: The Unknown Tennessee Williams*, is published by Crown Publishers.

1996   September 5: Rose Isabelle Williams dies in Tarrytown, New York.

        September 5: *The Notebook of Trigorin*, in a version revised by Williams, opens at the Cincinnati Playhouse in the Park.

1998   March 5: *Not About Nightingales* premieres at the Royal National Theatre in London, directed by Trevor Nunn, later moves to Houston, Texas, and opens November 25, 1999, on Broadway.

1999   November: *Spring Storm* is published.

2000   May: *Stairs to the Roof* is published.

        November: *The Selected Letters of Tennessee Williams, Volume I* is published.

2001   June: *Fugitive Kind* is published.

2002   April: *Collected Poems* is published.

2004   August: *Candles to the Sun* is published.

November: *The Selected Letters of Tennessee Williams, Volume II* is published.

2005   April: *Mister Paradise and Other One-Act Plays* is published.

2008   April: *A House Not Meant to Stand* and *The Traveling Companion and Other Plays* are published.

May 20: Walter Dakin Williams dies at the age of 89 in Belleville, Illinois.